Vita Contemplativa

Byung-Chul Han

Vita Contemplativa
In Praise of Inactivity

Translated by Daniel Steuer

polity

Originally published in German as *Vita Contemplativa. Oder von der Untätigkeit* © by Ullstein Buchverlage GmbH, Berlin. Published in 2022 by Ullstein Verlag.

This English edition © Polity Press, 2024

Excerpt from Paul Celan's *Selected Poems*, tr. Michael Hamburger © Penguin Random House, 1996. Reproduced with permission of Johnson & Alcock Ltd.

Polity Press
65 Bridge Street
Cambridge CB2 1UR, UK

Polity Press
111 River Street
Hoboken, NJ 07030, USA

ISBN-13: 978-1-5095-5800-1 – hardback
ISBN-13: 978-1-5095-5801-8 – paperback

A catalogue record for this book is available from the British Library.

Library of Congress Control Number: 2023934603

Typeset in 11pt on 15pt Janson Text
by Cheshire Typesetting Ltd, Cuddington, Cheshire
Printed and bound in by Great Britain by CPI Group (UK) Ltd, Croydon

The publisher has used its best endeavours to ensure that the URLs for external websites referred to in this book are correct and active at the time of going to press. However, the publisher has no responsibility for the websites and can make no guarantee that a site will remain live or that the content is or will remain appropriate.

Every effort has been made to trace all copyright holders, but if any have been overlooked the publisher will be pleased to include any necessary credits in any subsequent reprint or edition.

For further information on Polity, visit our website:
politybooks.com

CONTENTS

You
you teach
you teach your hands
you teach your hands you teach
you teach your hands
                    to sleep

Paul Celan
('Matière de Bretagne', in *Selected Poems*,
London: Penguin, 1996, p. 127)

                              We are such stuff
As dreams are made on, and our little life
Is rounded with a sleep.

William Shakespeare
(*The Tempest*, Act 4, Scene 1, ll. 156–8
New Haven: Yale University Press, 2006, p. 107)

I gave up before birth.

Samuel Beckett
(*Fizzles 4*, in *The Complete Short Prose 1929–1989*,
New York: Grove Press, 1995, pp. 234ff)

Views of Inactivity

We increasingly resemble the sort of active people who 'roll as the stone rolls, in obedience to the stupidity of the laws of mechanics'.[1] Because we look at life exclusively from the perspective of work and performance, we view inactivity as a deficiency that must be overcome as quickly as possible. Human existence is fully absorbed by activity, and thereby becomes exploitable. We are losing a sense for the kind of inactivity that is not an incapability, not a refusal, not just the absence of activity but a capacity in itself. Inactivity has a logic of its own, its own language, temporality, architecture, magnificence – even its own magic. It is not a weakness or defect but rather an *intensity*, which is, however, neither seen nor acknowledged in our active and performance-driven society. We cannot access the riches of the realm of inactivity. Inactivity is a *radiance* within human existence. Today, it has paled into an *emptiness* within activity.

Under capitalist relations of production, inactivity returns in the form of an *encapsulated outside*. We call it 'leisure time'. Because it serves the purpose of respite from work, it remains tied to the logic of work. As *derivative of work*, it represents a functional element of production. What thus disappears is *free time* that does not belong to the order of work and production. We no longer know the holy, festive calmness 'that unites intensity of life with contemplation, and is still able to unite them even when intensity of life grows into exuberance'.[2] 'Leisure time' lacks both intensity of life and contemplation. It is a time that we kill so as not to get bored. It is not *free, living time*; it is *dead time*. Intense life today means first of all more performance or more consumption. We have forgotten that it is precisely inactivity, which does not produce anything, that represents an intense and radiant form of life. To oppose the compulsion of work and performance, we must create a *politics of inactivity* that is able to produce genuinely *free time*.

Inactivity constitutes the *human*. The inactivity involved in any doing is what makes the doing something genuinely human. Without moments of pause or hesitation, acting deteriorates into blind action and reaction. Without calm, a new barbarism emerges. Silence deepens conversation. Without stillness, there is no music – just sound and noise. Play is the essence of beauty. When life follows the rule of stimulus–response, need–satisfaction and goal–action, it atrophies into pure survival: naked biological life. Life receives its radiance only from inactivity. If we lose the ability to be inactive, we begin to resemble machines that must simply *function*. True life begins when concern for survival, for the exigencies of mere life, ends. The ultimate purpose of all human endeavour is inactivity.

Action constitutes history, but it is not a force that forms culture. The origin of culture is not war but the festival, not the weapon but the adornment. History and culture are not congruent. Culture is formed by diversion, excess and detour; it is not produced by following the path that leads straight to the goal. The essence at the core of culture is *ornamentation*. Culture sits beyond functionality and usefulness. The ornamental dimension, emancipated from any goal or use, is how life insists that it is more than survival. Life receives its divine radiance from that *absolute decoration* that does not adorn anything. 'To point out that the baroque is decorative does not say everything about it. It is *decorazione assoluta*, as if it had emancipated itself from every purpose, even the theatrical, and developed its own law of form. It ceases to decorate anything and is, on the contrary, nothing but decoration.'[3]

During the Sabbath, all activity must cease. No business may be pursued. Essential to the Sabbath are inactivity and the suspension of economic life. Capitalism, by contrast, turns even the festival into a commodity. It becomes an event and a spectacle that lacks contemplative calmness. As a form of consumption, it does not found community. In his essay *The Society of the Spectacle*, Guy Debord states that contemporary time is one without festivals:

Although the present age presents its time to itself as a series of frequently recurring festivities, it is an age that knows nothing of real festivals. The moments within

3

cyclical time when members of a community joined together in a luxurious expenditure of life are impossible for a society that lacks both community and luxury.[4]

An epoch without the festival is an epoch without community. Today, people frequently invoke the term 'community', but in doing so they refer to a commodified form of society.[5] It does not create a *we*. Unbridled consumption isolates and separates people. Consumers are lonely creatures. Digital communication, too, turns out to be a form of communication without community. Social media accelerates the disintegration of community. Capitalism transforms time itself into a commodity. In this way, time loses its festiveness. Debord remarks on the commercialization of time: 'The reality of time has been replaced by the publicity of time.'[6]

Another essential characteristic of the festival is luxury. Luxury suspends economic compulsion. As increased vitality, as an intensity, it is luxation, that is, deviation from the necessities and needs of mere life. Capitalism, by contrast, accords absolute value to survival. When life degenerates into survival, luxury disappears. Even the highest level of performance does not achieve luxury. Work and performance belong to the order of survival. Action does not take the form of luxury because action springs from a lack. In capitalism, even luxury is consumed; it takes on the form of a commodity and loses its festiveness and radiance.

For Theodor W. Adorno, luxury is emblematic of an uncorrupted happiness that is destroyed by the logic of efficiency. Efficiency and functionality are ways of survival. Luxury suspends them:

Rampant technology eliminates luxury . . . The express train that in three nights and two days hurtles across the continent is a miracle, but travelling in it has nothing of the faded splendour of the *train bleu*. What made up the voluptuousness of travel, beginning with the goodbye-waving through the open window, the solicitude of amiable accepters of tips, the ceremonial of mealtimes, the constant feeling of receiving favours that take nothing from anyone else, has passed away, together with the elegant people who were wont to promenade along the platforms before the departure, and who will by now be sought in vain even in the foyers of the most prestigious hotels.[7]

We owe true happiness to the useless and purposeless, to what is intentionally convoluted, what is unproductive, indirect, exuberant, superfluous, to beautiful forms and gestures that have no use and serve no purpose. Unlike walking to a destination, running somewhere or marching, taking a leisurely stroll is a luxury. *Ceremonious inactivity* means: *we do something, but to no end*. This 'to-no-end', this freedom from purpose and usefulness, is the essential core of inactivity. It is the basic formula for happiness.

Walter Benjamin's figure of the flâneur is characterized by inactivity: 'The peculiar irresolution of the flâneur. Just as waiting seems to be the proper state of the impassive thinker, doubt appears to be that of the flâneur. An elegy by Schiller contains the phrase: "the hesitant wing of the butterfly".'[8] Waiting and doubting are forms of inactivity. Without moments of doubt, our walk turns into a march. Like the wing of a butterfly, the human gait owes its grace to moments of hesitation, and resolution or haste deprive it of such grace. A flâneur makes use of the capacity *not to act*. He does not pursue a goal. Without an aim, he delivers himself to the space that twinkles at him, to 'the magnetism of the streetcorner, of a distant square in the fog, of the back of a woman walking before him'.[9]

Festivals are opposed to work insofar as they are altogether liberated from any 'in-order-to', from the kinds of purpose or usefulness to which work is subjugated. Freedom from 'in-order-to' affords human existence festiveness and radiance. The human gait, for instance, liberated from the 'in-order-to', from goal-oriented walking-towards, becomes a dance: 'but what is dance other than the liberation of the body from its utilitarian movements, the exhibition of gestures in their pure inoperativity?'[10] Likewise, hands, when liberated from the 'in-order-to', no longer *grasp*. They *play*. Or they form *pure gestures* that *do not indicate anything*.

When liberated from its practical uses, fire stimulates our imagination. It becomes a medium of inactivity.

> The fire confined to the fireplace was no doubt for man the first object of reverie, the symbol of repose, the invitation to repose. ... Thus, in our opinion, to be deprived of a reverie before a burning fire is to lose the first use and the truly human use of fire. ... one only receives comfort from the fire when one leans his elbows on his knees and holds his head in his hands. This attitude comes from the distant past. The child by the fire assumes it naturally. Not for nothing is it the attitude of the Thinker. It leads to a very special kind of attention which has nothing in common with the

attention involved in watching or observing. . . . When near the fire, one must be seated; one must rest without sleeping.[11]

Fire is usually associated with Promethean passion, with deed and action. Bachelard's psychoanalysis of fire, by contrast, uncovers its contemplative dimension. The posture that human beings, even children, intuitively adopt before a fire illustrates their age-old inclination towards contemplation. Contemplative inactivity is what distinguishes a thinker from a guardian or observer who always pursues a particular goal. A thinker, by contrast, *lacks all intention*, has *no goal in sight*.

In *Questiones Convivales*, Plutarch describes a ritual for exorcizing ravenousness (*bulímu exélasis*).[12] In Agamben's reading, this ritual serves the purpose of 'expelling a certain form of eating (devouring or engorging like wild beasts in order to satiate a hunger that is by definition insatiable), and thus clearing a space for another modality of eating, one that is human and festive, one that can begin only once the "hunger of an ox" has been expelled'.[13] Festivals are free from the needs of mere life. Eating becomes contemplative: 'Eating, in this respect, is not a *melachah*, an activity directed toward an aim, but an inoperativity and *menuchah*, a Sabbath of nourishment.'[14]

Ritual practices, in which inactivity plays a major role, elevate us above mere life. Fasting and asceticism explicitly distance themselves from living as survival, from the needs and necessities of mere life. They represent a kind of luxury, and this affords them a festive character. They are characterized by contemplative calmness. For Benjamin, fasting initiates us into the 'secrets of food'.[15] Fasting

7

sharpens the senses, so that they discover secret scents in even the most unexceptional food. When Benjamin involuntarily entered into a state of fasting while in Rome, he felt 'that here was an unrepeatable opportunity to unleash my senses into the folds and gorges of the most unassuming raw fruit and vegetables, melons, wine, ten varieties of bread or nuts, so as to identify a scent I had never before known'.[16] Ritual fasting *renews* life by enlivening the senses. It gives back to life its vitality, its radiance. Under the imperative of health, however, fasting puts itself in the service of survival. It loses its contemplative, festive dimension, and has to optimize naked life for its better functioning. Even fasting can in this way take on the form of survival.

Inactivity as such is *spiritual fasting*, and it therefore has a healing effect. The compulsion of production transforms inactivity into a form of activity in order to exploit it. Thus, even sleep is these days regarded as an activity. The so-called 'power nap' is an activity of sleep.[17] Even dreams are turned into a resource. The technique of 'lucid dreaming' is used to optimize physical and mental abilities during sleep. We extend the compulsion of performance and optimization even into our sleep. It is possible that in the future humans will abolish both sleep and dreams on the grounds of inefficiency.

'For a long time I would go to bed early' is the famous opening sentence of Marcel Proust's *A la recherche du temps perdu*. 'Early' translates the French expression 'de bonne heure': 'Longtemps, je me suis couché de bonne heure.' Sleep introduces the hour of happiness (*bonheur*). With sleep begins 'that more truthful hour when my eyes closed to the things of the outer world'.[18] Sleep is a *medium of truth*. We see the truth only once we enter into inactivity. Sleep reveals a true internal world that lies behind the things of the external world, which are mere semblance. The dreamer delves into the deeper layers of being. Proust believed that the inner life continuously weaves new threads between events, and creates a dense texture of relations in which nothing exists in isolation. Truth is a relational process. Everywhere it creates *similarities*. Truth takes place the moment a writer 'takes two different objects, states the connexion between them . . . truth – and life too – can be attained by us only when, by comparing a quality common to two sensations, we succeed in extracting their common essence and in reuniting them to each other, liberated from the contingencies of time within a metaphor'.[19]

Sleep and dreams are privileged places for truth. They suspend the separations and delimitations that dominate wakefulness. Things reveal their truth 'in that thoroughly alive and creative sleep of the unconscious (a sleep in which the things that have barely touched us succeed in carving an impression, in which our sleeping hands take hold of the key that turns the lock, the key for which we have sought in vain)'.[20] Activity and action are blind to truth. They touch only the surface of things. Hands that are determined to act will not find the key to the truth. That key falls into the hands of the sleeper.

Proust's *In Search of Lost Time* is one drawn-out dream. The *mémoire involontaire* is an epiphany, a source of happiness, and as such it is at home in the realm of inactivity. It resembles a door that opens as if by magic. Happiness does not belong to the order of knowledge or causality. It has something of sorcery and magic about it:

9

But it is sometimes just at the moment when we think that everything is lost that the intimation arrives which may save us; one has knocked at all the doors which lead nowhere, and then one stumbles without knowing it on the only door through which one can enter – which one might have sought in vain for a hundred years – and it opens of its own accord.[21]

Sleep and boredom are states of inactivity. Sleep is the highest point of physical relaxation, whereas boredom is the highest point of mental relaxation. Benjamin calls boredom a 'warm gray fabric lined on the inside with the most lustrous and colourful of silks', and 'in this fabric we wrap ourselves when we dream'.[22] Boredom is 'the dream bird that hatches the egg of experience'.[23] That bird's nests, however, are rapidly falling apart, and thus 'the gift of listening is lost'.[24]

Experience in the genuine sense does not arise out of work and performance. It cannot be created through activity. Rather, it presupposes a particular form of passivity and inactivity: 'To undergo an experience with something – be it a thing, a person, or a god – means that this something befalls us, strikes us, comes over us, overwhelms and transforms us.'[25] Experience is due to a giving and receiving. Its medium is *listening*. But the noise of contemporary information and communication puts an end to the 'community of listeners'.[26] No one is *listening*; everyone is *playing to the gallery*.

Inactivity is time-consuming. It requires a *long whiling*, an intense, contemplative lingering.[27] In an era of rushing, in which everything is short term, short of breath and short-sighted, it is rare. Today, the consumerist form of life prevails everywhere. In this form of life, every need must be satisfied *at once*. We are *impatient* if we are told to *wait* for something to slowly *ripen*. All that matter are short-term effects and quick gains. Actions are reduced to reactions. Experiences are diluted, and become events. Feelings are impoverished, and become emotions or affects. We have no access to reality – reality reveals itself only to contemplative attention.

We are becoming ever less able to endure boredom, so our ability to have experiences is withering. The dream bird is already threatened with extinction in the analogue world of rustling newspaper leaves: 'In the woods of illustrated journals he [the dream bird] must perish. And he also no longer has a home in what we do. . . . the leisure that gave humans creating hands has become extinct'.[28] The creating hand *does not act. It listens.* The internet, where we cannot see the wood for the digital trees, robs us of the 'gift of listening'. The dream bird that hatches the egg of experience resembles motionless contemplation. While waiting, it surrenders to an 'unconscious process'. To an external view, it appears inactive. But this inactivity is the condition of the possibility of experience.

Waiting begins only once it is no longer a waiting for something specific. When we expect something specific, we wait less, and close ourselves off from the *unconscious process*: 'Waiting begins when there is nothing left to wait for, not even the end of waiting itself. Waiting ignores and destroys what it is waiting for. Waiting waits for nothing.'[29] Waiting is the mental attitude of the one who is contemplatively inactive. To such a person, an altogether different reality is revealed, one to which no activity, no action, has access.

Waiting also determines Orpheus's relation to Eurydice. Only in waiting is he close to Eurydice. He can sing for her, desire her, but not possess her. Her withdrawal is the condition of the possibility of his singing. Eurydice disappears irretrievably the very moment that Orpheus, worried that she might no longer be following him, turns around to assure himself of her presence. Eurydice embodies the realm of inactivity, night, shadow, sleep and death. It is fundamentally impossible to bring her into daylight. Orpheus owes his song, his work (*œuvre*), precisely to death, which is nothing other than the *utmost intensification of inactivity*. Blanchot places *desœuvrement*, meaning inactivity – literally de-working or worklessness – close to death. Night, sleep and death turn Orpheus into the one who is 'inert, "désoeuvré"', the one who is 'out of work'.[30] Artists owe their gift of listening, the gift of narration, to inactivity, to *desœuvrement*. Orpheus is the primordial artist. Art requires an intensive relation to death. Only in *being towards death* does the *literary space* open up. Writing is always *writing towards death*: 'Kafka is in a sense already dead. This is given him . . . and this gift is linked to that of writing.'[31]

Knowledge cannot represent life in its totality. The *fully known* life is a dead life. Whatever is alive is not *transparent* to itself. It is precisely not-knowing, as a form of inactivity, that *enlivens* life. In an aphorism from the phase of the so-called 'new enlightenment', Nietzsche declares ignorance to be the *nucleus of life*:

It is not enough to recognize the ignorance in which man and beast live; you must realize that they are, and you yourself must be, determined to be ignorant. You need to understand that without this kind of ignorance life itself would be impossible, that only under this condition can a living thing survive and thrive: a great solid globe of ignorance must surround you.[32]

The determined will to knowledge misses the innermost and deepest dimension of life. It paralyses vitality. Nietzsche would also say that life is impossible without inactivity, that it is the condition under which what lives preserves itself and flourishes.

In Kleist's 'On the Marionette Theatre', grace comes from ignorance, involuntariness and inactivity. The human dancer can never be as graceful as the marionettes, which 'in their own fashion' follow only the 'simple law of gravity'.[33] Rather than moving voluntarily, they hover above the ground. Their movements happen as if 'by themselves'.[34] In this way, they owe their grace to a not-doing-anything. It is precisely conscious and voluntary doing that robs movements of their grace. Kleist's text also tells the story of a young man who loses his gracefulness the moment that, seeing himself in the mirror, he becomes *aware* of his posture. Grace and beauty lie beyond conscious effort: 'We can see the degree to which contemplation becomes darker and weaker in the organic world, so that the grace that is there emerges all the more shining and triumphant.'[35]

The ultimate aim of practice is to reach a state in which the will abdicates. The master *exercises the will away*. A *not-doing* is the essence of masterly skill. Activity reaches perfection in inactivity. The *happy hand* lacks will and consciousness. Of practice, Walter Benjamin writes:

To weary the master to the point of exhaustion through diligence and hard work, so that at long last his body and each of his limbs can act in accordance with their own rationality: this is what is called 'practice.' It is successful because the will abdicates its power once and for all inside the body, abdicates in favor of the organs – the hand, for instance. This is why you can look for something for days, until you finally forget it; then, one day, when you are looking for something else, you suddenly find the first object. Your hand has, so to speak, taken the matter in hand and has joined forces with the object.[36]

The will frequently blinds us to what is *happening*. By illuminating what is *happening*, illuminating *being* at a point that precedes both will and consciousness, unintentionality and involuntariness make us clear-sighted.

In a short sketch titled 'Do Not Forget the Best', Benjamin presents a parable of a happy life. The protagonist is an active man who engages in his 'current activities' with determination and diligence. He registers everything down to the smallest detail. When he has an appointment, he is 'punctuality itself'. In his routines, there is 'not even the smallest crack for time to run out of control'. He thus has no *free* time. His busy life is, however, extremely unhappy. Then something unexpected happens, and it brings about a radical change in his existence. He throws away his watch, and practises being late. Only once 'the person he was going to meet had already left, he sat down to wait'. At this point, joyous things come to him unbidden, without him doing anything. The paths of heaven reveal themselves to him: 'Friends visited him when he least expected them but needed them most,

14

and the gifts he sent, which were not sumptuous, arrived at just the right time, as if he had the paths of heaven in his hands.' The protagonist recalls the tale of the shepherd boy who '*one Sunday*' was given permission to enter the mountain containing rich treasures, receiving the mysterious instruction, 'Do not forget the best'. The best is *not-doing*. Benjamin's parable of inactivity ends with the words: 'At this period in his life, he felt quite well. He got few things, and considered nothing as done.'[37]

Those who are genuinely inactive do not affirm *themselves*. They give up their names and become *no one*. *Nameless and intentionless*, they succumb to what *happens*. Roland Barthes comes across the 'idleness [he] dream[s] about' in a haiku:

Sitting peacefully doing nothing
Springtime is coming
and the grass grows all by itself.

Barthes points out that the haiku contains an important anacoluthon, a grammatical break. The one sitting peacefully, doing nothing, is not the actual subject of the sentence. The subject gives up his grammatical place and disappears in favour of springtime as subject: 'Springtime is coming'. Barthes concludes from this that 'in a situation of idleness the subject is almost dispossessed of his consistency as a subject'. The subject is constituted by activity and action; an inactive subject is an absurdity. Subject and action condition each other. Inactivity (Barthes calls it 'idleness' or 'laziness') has a de-subjectifying, de-individualizing, even *disarming* effect. Grass, the other subject of the sentence, also highlights inactivity as the haiku's *overall mood*. The grass grows 'all by itself'. To continue Barthes's thought, the passion of inactivity brings about a *psychological anacoluthon*. The subject gives itself up. It surrenders *itself* to what is *happening*. Every action, every activity, is suspended in favour of a *subjectless taking-place*: 'That would be true idleness. To be able, at certain moments, to no longer have to say "I".'[38]

A master of contemplation is characterized by a *mimetic faculty*. He moves into things by making himself *similar* to them. In *Berlin Childhood around 1900*, Benjamin tells the story of a Chinese painter who disappears into his painting in front of his friends' eyes:

> The story comes from China, and tells of an old painter who invited friends to see his newest picture. This picture showed a park and a narrow footpath that ran along a stream and through a grove of trees, culminating at the door of a little cottage in the background. When the painter's friends, however, looked around for the painter, they saw that he was gone – that he was in the picture. There, he followed the little path that led to the door, paused before it quite still, turned, smiled, and disappeared through the narrow opening. In the same way, I too, when occupied with my paintpots and brushes, would be suddenly displaced into the picture. I would resemble the porcelain which I had entered in a cloud of colors.[39]

Before finally disappearing altogether, the painter *smiles*. Benjamin interprets his smile as a mimetic faculty. It represents the 'highest level of mimetic openness'. It signals the preparedness 'to make oneself similar to the one at which it is directed'. The *magic smile* indicates 'mastery of mimesis in the form of adaptive metamorphosis'.[40] The mimetic condition is a *condition of self-lessness* that makes possible a playful *transition towards the other*. The *friendliness of the smile* is its essential trait.

Inactivity is not the opposite of activity. Rather, activity feeds off inactivity. Benjamin raises inactivity to the position of midwife to the new: 'We are bored when we don't know what we are waiting for. That we do know, or think we know, is nearly always the expression of our superficiality or inattention. Boredom is the threshold to great deeds.'[41] Boredom constitutes the 'external surface of unconscious events'.[42] Without it, nothing *takes place*. The seed of the new is not the determination to act but the unconscious event. When we lose the capacity to experience boredom, we also lose access to the activities that rest on it: 'Boredom, however, no longer has a place in our lives. The activities that were secretly and intimately connected with boredom are dying out.'[43]

The *dialectic of inactivity* transforms inactivity into a threshold, a zone of indeterminacy that enables us to create something that was *not there before*. Without this threshold, the same keeps repeating itself. Thus Nietzsche writes:

'Inventive people live *altogether differently* from active ones; they need *time*, so that purposeless, unregulated activity occurs, experiments can take place, and new paths can be taken; they feel their way, rather than walking just on the old paths, as the usefully active people do.'[44]

Those who are creatively active differ from those who are usefully active to the extent that their doing is *for nothing.* It is the *proportion of inactivity in their activity* that makes possible the emergence of something *altogether different*, something that has never *been there before.*

Only silence enables us to say something *unheard of.* The compulsion of communication, by contrast, leads to the reproduction of the same, to conformism:

> So it's not a problem of getting people to express themselves but of providing little gaps of solitude and silence in which they might eventually find something to say. Repressive forces don't stop people expressing themselves but rather force them to express themselves. What a relief to have nothing to say, the right to say nothing, because only then is there a chance of framing the rare, and ever rarer, thing that might be worth saying.[45]

The compulsion of activity perpetuates the same in a similar way. Only the open spaces of inactivity enable us to bring about what is increasingly rare: something that actually deserves *to be done.* In this way, inactivity is the threshold to an *unheard-of deed.*

The compulsion to be active, the acceleration of life, turns out to be an efficient means of rule. If revolution is inconceivable today, that may be because we do not have time to think. Without time, without catching a deep breath, the same continues. The free spirit perishes:

> Because time for thinking and quietness in thinking are lacking, one no longer ponders deviant views: one contents oneself with hating them. With the tremendous acceleration of life mind and eye have become accustomed to seeing and judging partially or inaccurately,

and everyone is like the traveller who gets to know a land and its people from a railway carriage. An independent and cautious attitude towards knowledge is disparaged almost as a kind of derangement, the free spirit is brought into disrepute.[46]

Having voiced his complaint about the ruling conformism, Nietzsche continues: 'Such a lament as has just been sung will probably one day have had its time and, when the genius of meditation makes a mighty reappearance, fall silent of its own volition.'[47] Nietzsche mentions that 'at no time have the active, that is to say the restless, counted for more', and that as a result 'our civilization is turning into a new barbarism'. Therefore, 'one of the most necessary corrections to the character of mankind that have to be taken in hand is a considerable strengthening of the contemplative element in it'.[48]

When the compulsion of production takes hold of language, language enters the mode of work. It withers and becomes a bearer of information, that is, merely a means of communication. Information is the *active form of language*. Poetry, by contrast, suspends language as information. In poetry, language enters the mode of contemplation. It becomes inactive:

Because poetry is precisely . . . the point at which language, which has deactivated its communicative and informative functions, rests within itself, contemplates its power of saying [*potenza di dire*] and in this way opens itself to a new possible use. In this way, Dante's *La Vita Nuova* and Leopardi's *Canti* are the contemplation of the Italian language.[49]

19

As active persons, we rarely read poetry any more. The loss of the faculty of contemplation affects our relation to language. Dazed by the rush of information and communication, we move away from poetry as the contemplation of language, and begin even to hate it.

When language is nothing but work and the production of information, it loses its radiance. It becomes worn out, and keeps reproducing the same. The French writer Michel Butor says that the current crisis of literature is a result of communication: 'For ten or twenty years, almost nothing has happened in literature. There is a flood of publications, but intellectual stasis. The cause is a crisis of communication. The new means of communication are admirable, but they produce an enormous noise.'[50] Communicative noise destroys *silence*, robs language of its contemplative capacity. For this reason, language cannot reach new expressive possibilities.

Capital is the *pure form of activity*. It is the transcendence that takes hold of the immanence of life and exploits it completely. From life, it separates bare life, life that *works*. The human being is degraded into an *animal laborans*. Freedom is exploited, too. According to Marx, free competition is nothing but 'the relation of capital to itself as another capital'.[51] While we compete freely with each other, capital multiplies. Only capital is truly free: 'It is not individuals who are set free by free competition; it is, rather, capital which is set free.'[52] The individuals who imagine that they are free are essentially the sexual organs of capital, the means of its procreation. The neoliberal excess of freedom and performance is simply an excess of capital.

The *politics of inactivity* liberates the immanence of life from the transcendence that alienates life from itself. Only in inactivity do we become aware of the ground on which we rest, and of the space in which we are. Life enters the contemplative mode, and swings back to its secret foundation in being. It finds itself and looks at itself. It reaches its deep immanence. Only inactivity initiates us into the secret of life.

For Deleuze, the immanence of life is bliss:

> We will say of pure immanence that it is A LIFE, and nothing else. It is not immanence to life, but the immanent that is in nothing is itself a life. A life is . . . absolute immanence: it is complete power, complete bliss.[53]

Immanence as life is *living in the mode of contemplation*. Life as immanence is a capacity that does *not act*. It is an 'immanent that is in nothing', because it is not subjected to anything and is not dependent on anything. Life relates to itself and rests in itself. Immanence denotes a life that possesses itself, that suffices itself. This self-sufficiency is bliss. It characterizes those small children who, in their inactivity, seem almost to radiate: 'Small children, through all their sufferings and weaknesses, are infused with an immanent life that is pure power and even bliss.'[54] This 'pure power' expresses itself in the form of 'a pure contemplation without knowledge' (*pure contemplation sans connaissance*), as 'silent contemplations'.[55]

Deleuze's children, full of 'immanent life', resemble Handke's 'small children' who happily lose themselves in inactivity: 'and every evening here in Linares I watched

21

the growing tiredness of the many small children . . .
no more greed, no grabbing hold of things, only play-
fulness'.[56] The 'fundamental', 'ethereal tiredness'[57] that
Handke invoked in his 'Essay on Tiredness' is reflected
in the 'pure power' that does *not act*:

> So let's have a Pindaric ode, not to a victor but to a
> tired man. I conceive of the Pentecostal company that
> received the Holy Ghost as tired to a man. The inspira-
> tion of tiredness tells them not so much what should, as
> what need not, be done.[58]

Handke's 'ethereal tiredness' differs from the profane
tiredness of impotence, which is the inability to do something. As *pure power*, it does not submit to any *in-order-to*,
any purpose or aim. The tired person does something,
but *for nothing*. The tired person resembles a child who
is constantly moving without *getting anything done* or
accomplished.

In a passage of *The Man without Qualities*, Musil imagi-
nes a *realm of inactivity*, an *eternal Sabbath*. An 'enchanted
spirit of inaction'[59] leads the world into a state of
contemplation:

> 'You must keep quite still . . . You must also shed the
> judiciousness with which you perform tasks. You must
> deprive the mind of all tools and not allow it to be used
> as a tool. . . . You must keep to yourself until head, heart,
> and limbs are nothing but silence. But if, in this way,
> you attain the highest selflessness, then finally outer and
> inner will touch each other as if a wedge that had split
> the world had popped out!'[60]

Musil's 'day-bright mysticism' creates an 'other condition'.[61] It suspends the distinctions that isolate things from one another. Things flow into each other, as in a 'dream state'.[62] The *landscape of inactivity* is without separating borders. Things unite and reconcile themselves with each other: 'Let me put it this way: the details no longer have their egoism, which they use to capture our attention, but they're all linked with each other in a familiar, literally "inward" way.'[63]

'Ethereal tiredness' signifies spirit in the mode of contemplation. To the gaze of the tired person, the world is revealed in its state of reconciliation. 'All in one' is the formula of reconciliation:

> The other becomes I. Those two children down there before my eyes are also I. And the way the older sister is dragging her little brother through the room has a meaning and a value, and nothing is worth more than anything else – the rain falling on the tired man's wrist is worth as much as his view of the people walking on the other side of the river, both are good and beautiful, and that is as it should be, now and forever – and above all it is true.[64]

The deeper meaning of truth is the shared *mood* [Überein-Stimmung] between things. Truth and beauty converge in friendliness. In the *landscape of inactivity*, things are wedded to each other. The landscape *shines. Spirit in the mode of inactivity* is *shining*:

> Cézanne almost always creates the marriage – the wedding – of everything to everything: the tree becomes

23

rain, the air becomes stone, one thing strives towards the other: the smile in the earth's landscape.[65]

In the *landscape of inactivity*, nothing delineates itself from any other thing. Nothing rests in itself or clings on to itself. The 'odor of the pines which is harsh in the sun, must marry the . . . odor of the stones, and of marble from Saint-Victoire in the distance'.[66] The shining friendliness that floods through Cézanne's *landscape of inactivity* arises from the symphony of things: 'All the colour tones pervade each other, all the forms stir as they slot into each other. Here, there is continuity.'[67] Things enter into frank relations with one another: 'These glasses, these dishes, they talk among themselves.'[68] The aim of painting is nothing but 'to discover the amity of all these things in the open air'.[69] Painting expresses the *shared mood of things*, that is, their *truth*. Sharp distinctions and stark contrasts that set things off from each other are surface phenomena: in the deep layers of being, they are suspended.

What destroys the *continuity of being* is human intention and judgement. Cézanne writes: 'Why do we divide the world? Is it a reflection of our egotism? We want everything to serve us.'[70] For things to shine in their own light, liberated from human intentions and actions, which submit things to us, human beings have to hold themselves back: 'We live in the midst of man-made objects, among tools, in houses, streets, cities, and most of the time we see them only *through the human actions* which put them to use.'[71] Cézanne's *landscape of inactivity* cuts ties with humanized nature, and restores *an order of things that is not anthropomorphic*, in which things can be themselves again. Cézanne's apples, for instance, are *not fit for consumption*. His jugs and plates are not 'ware' [*Zeug*], not tools that are subjected to an in-order-to – to human purposes. Rather, they have their own dignity, their own radiance.

The ideal painter does away with activity and volition, and lets everything happen by itself. The painting succeeds when the painter becomes *no one*: 'Well, no one has ever painted the landscape, man absent but entirely within the landscape.'[72] The painter paints himself *away*, loses himself in the landscape. He transposes the landscape 'unconsciously' on to the canvas.[73] The unbounded landscape moves into the tip of the brush and paints itself. Cézanne's call for inactivity says: *make silence*. The *noisy I* and its will, its intentions and inclinations, must be made to disappear. On the task of the painter, Cézanne remarks: 'His entire will must be silent. He must silence all prejudice within himself. He must forget, forget, be quiet, be a perfect echo. Then the full landscape will inscribe itself on his photographic plate.'[74]

For Cézanne, inactivity is the ideal form of human existence. His paintings are suffused with an *ethos of inactivity*. A commentary on the series of paintings called 'The Card Players' says: 'Cézanne shows the peasants while playing or inactive, with their hands in their laps . . . leaving superficial socialism behind, he points ahead towards an ultimate liberation of humans from work, hardship, and burdens.'[75] The series 'The Bathers' presents a *utopia of inactivity*. Humans and nature fuse in the radiance of inactivity. They penetrate each other. In some cases, the bathers literally flow into the landscape. There is no action, no intention, that separates

25

humans from nature. 'The Bathers' shows the world in the state of redemption. The reconciliation between humans and nature is the final purpose of a *politics of inactivity*.

A Marginal Note on Zhuangzi

In an anecdote that reads like a continuation of Kleist's 'On the Marionette Theatre', Zhuangzi tells the story of a cook who is a master of inactivity. He practises doing nothing. Rather than wilfully intervening in things, he makes use of the *possibilities* that lie dormant in them. He butchers oxen by inserting his knife in the various spaces made by the joints. A good cook, he explains, hardly ever has to change his knife, because he *cuts*. A bungling cook, by contrast, has to change his knife very often, because he *chops* with maximum force. Zhuangzi's cook cuts up oxen effortlessly:

> I size up the difficulties, tell myself to watch out and be careful, keep my eyes on what I'm doing, work very slowly, and move the knife with the greatest subtlety, until – flop! the whole thing comes apart like a clod of earth crumbling to the ground.[1]

Zhuangzi describes butchery as a *process free of compulsion and intention*. His cook is, in fact, inactive. *He is simply present at the process*, which he, so to speak, nudges into existence. After the ox has fallen apart as if by itself, the cook is astounded by the miraculous event that took place without his involvement.

The famous pioneer of natural farming Masanobu Fukuoka rigorously applied Zhuangzi's teachings. He called his method 'doing-nothing farming'. He was convinced that modern agricultural techniques destroy the subtle laws of nature. They offer solutions, but only for the problems that they themselves create. Farming by way of inactivity makes use of the forces that are already present in nature, just as Zhuangzi's cook does. As Zhuangzi might have put it: *the wise farmer does not plough*. Indeed, Fukuoka's do-nothing farming forgoes the plough:

The first [principle of doing-nothing farming] is NO CULTIVATION, that is, no ploughing or turning of the soil. For Centuries, farmers have assumed that the plough is essential for growing crops. However, non-cultivation is fundamental to natural farming. The earth cultivates itself naturally by means of the penetration of plant roots and the activity of microorganisms, small animals, and earthworms. ... People interfere with nature and, try as they may, they cannot heal the resulting wounds. ... If left to itself, the soil maintains its fertility naturally, in accordance with the orderly cycle of plant and animal life.[2]

Like Zhuangzi's cook, a good farmer sees his job as a letting happen. Doing-nothing is his ethos. Passages from

Fukuoka's writings sound like Zhuangzian parables: 'If a tree is planted carefully and allowed to follow the natural form from the beginning, there is no need for pruning or sprays of any kind.'[3]

Heidegger also comes close to Zhuangzi's philosophy of inactivity. Heidegger's 'releasement' has an element of doing-nothing. Humanity destroys the earth by tearing it out of its 'inconspicuous law of the possible'[4] and submitting it to total availability:

> It is first the will which arranges itself everywhere in technology that devours the earth in the exhaustion and consumption and change of what is artificial. Technology drives the earth beyond the developed sphere of its possibility into such things which are no longer a possibility and are thus the impossible.[5]

Saving the earth means: *leaving it within the possible, the developed sphere of its possibilities*. Heidegger's *ethics of inactivity* consists in making use of the *possible*, instead of imposing the impossible on it.

From Acting to Being

A Klee painting named *Angelus Novus* shows an angel looking as though he is about to move away from something he is fixedly contemplating. His eyes are staring, his mouth is open, his wings are spread. This is how one pictures the angel of history. His face is turned towards the past. Where we perceive a chain of events, he sees one single catastrophe which keeps piling wreckage upon wreckage and hurls it in front of his feet. The angel would like to stay, awaken the dead, and make whole what has been smashed. But a storm is blowing from Paradise; it has got caught in his wings with such violence that the angel can no longer close them. This storm irresistibly propels him into the future to which his back is turned, while the pile of debris before him grows skyward. This storm is what we call progress.

Walter Benjamin, *Theses on the Philosophy of History*[1]

Hannah Arendt considered the twentieth century an era of action. Even our relationship to nature is determined by action rather than wonder. Humans act beyond the social sphere by intervening in nature and submitting it to the human will. This unleashes processes that would not exist without human intervention. They lead to a complete loss of control:

> It is as if we had carried our own unpredictability – the fact that no one has a complete grasp of the consequences of their actions – into nature itself, thereby transposing the old natural law (in whose unconditional reliability we wanted to trust all the more because we ourselves are the unpredictable and never fully reliable ones par excellence) into the realm of the entirely different kind of laws that govern human actions, laws that are never universally valid and can never be unconditionally reliable.[2]

The Anthropocene is the result of the total submission of nature to human action. Nature loses all independence and dignity. It is reduced to a part of, an appendix to, human history. The lawfulness of nature is subjected to human wilfulness and to the unpredictability of human action. We *make* history by acting, and now we *make* nature by dissolving it into the contexts created by human action. The Anthropocene marks the precise moment that nature is completely absorbed into and exploited by human action.

What is to be done in the face of the catastrophic consequences of human action in nature? Arendt frankly admits that she has no solution. Her remarks, she says, seek only to encourage further reflection on 'the nature and the possibilities of the human capacity to act which has never before been so openly visible in its greatness and dangerousness'. She also wants to initiate a process of 'reflection' [*Besinnung*] whose 'end-result, in a possibly still far removed future, might be a philosophy of politics that is adequate for our times and experiences'.[3]

What kind of 'philosophy of politics' would lead to that 'reflection' on the full problematic involved in human action? A critical philosophy of action? In *The Human Condition*, Arendt presents human action first and foremost in its greatness and dignity. Action, in the strong sense, produces history. Here, the only dangerous aspect of human action for Arendt is the unpredictability of its consequences. Even later, she does not consider the possibility that it is precisely the superior status of human action, which she does not question, that is responsible for the catastrophes of which there were already unmistakeable signs during the time she was writing. The philosophy that is the still far off result of a fundamental process of reflection would need to have as its subject the human capacity *not to act*.

Acting is the verb that belongs to history. Walter Benjamin's *angel of history* is confronted with the catastrophic consequences of human action. In front of him, the debris of history piles up. But he cannot reduce it, because there is a storm, called 'progress', blowing from paradise, which pushes him on. His wide eyes and gaping mouth reflect his helplessness and horror. Human history is an ongoing apocalypse. It is, however, an *apocalypse free of events*. What is catastrophic is the *event-less continuation of what is now*:

32

The concept of progress must be grounded in the idea of catastrophe. That things are 'status quo' *is* the catastrophe. It is not an ever-present possibility but what in each case is given. . . . hell is not something that awaits us, but this life here and now.[4]

What is catastrophic is not the irruption of an unexpected event but the continuity of the 'on and on', the continual repetition of the same. Even the newest turns out to be the same again: 'It is rather that precisely in that which is newest the face of the world never alters, that this newest remains, in every respect, the same. – This constitutes the eternity of hell.'[5] What would save us would therefore be a radical *interruption of the now*. Only an *angel of inactivity* would be able to arrest the human action that inevitably becomes apocalyptic.

A couple of years before the publication of Arendt's *The Human Condition*, Martin Heidegger delivered a lecture titled 'Science and Reflection' [*Wissenschaft und Besinnung*]. Unlike action, which pushes forward, reflection leads us back to where we *always already* are. It opens up for us a *being-there* [*Da-Sein*] that precedes all doing, all action. It even *lingers ahead* of action. A dimension of inactivity is intrinsic to reflection. Reflection hands itself over to what *is*:

> To follow a direction that is the way that something has, of itself, already taken is called, in our language, sinnan, sinnen [to sense]. . . . It is calm, self-possessed surrender to that which is worthy of questioning.
>
> Through reflection so understood we actually arrive at the place where, without having experienced it and

without having seen penetratingly into it, we have long been sojourning. In reflection we gain access to a place from out of which there first opens the space traversed at any given time by all our doing and leaving undone.[6]

Reflection is a faculty that does *not act*. It implies that we stop and pause, as an *interruption, inactivity*. In one of the *Black Notebooks*, Heidegger asks: 'What if the presentiment of the silent power of *idle meditation* [*untätige Besinnung*] disappeared?'[7] Presentiment is not a deficient form of knowledge. Rather, it discloses *being* to us; it discloses the *there* that escapes propositional knowledge. Only by way of presentiment do we have access to that place where a human being always already is:

> Presentiment – taken in terms of the basic disposition, versus the ordinary, calculative understanding of it – does not at all concern merely the future, merely what is imminent, but instead traverses and measures up the whole of temporality: the temporal-spatial playing field of the 'there'.[8]

Presentiment is not an 'outer court before the gates of knowledge'. Rather, it provides access to that 'great hall' in which all that can be known has its place, that is, takes place.[9] Heidegger's thinking tirelessly circles that primordial *there* that cannot be captured in any form of propositional knowledge.

'Inactive reflection' aims at the *magic of the there* that escapes human action. Its steps 'do not lead forward but back, back to where we already are'.[10] They 'allow us to reach ... that domain where we are already staying'.[11]

The radical immanence of this *there* is *so close* that we constantly overlook it. It is the *'overly close'*, which is closer than the closest object. Someone who is only ever active will inevitably skip over it. It reveals itself only to inactive, contemplative lingering. Heidegger mobilizes an extensive vocabulary in connection with inactivity, so as to articulate the pre-propositional *there* in language. One element of this vocabulary is the motif of waiting: 'Waiting is a capacity that transcends all power to act. One who finds his way into the ability to wait surpasses all achieving and its accomplishments.'[12] Only once we wait, free of any intention, in waiting lingering, do humans become aware of the space in which we always already are: 'In waiting, the human-being [*das Menschenwesen*] becomes gathered in attentiveness to that in which he belongs.'[13] 'Inactive reflection' feels for the radiance of what is unprepossessing, what cannot be done, what is not available, what evades all usefulness and purpose: 'The poverty of reflection is the promise of a wealth whose treasures glow in the resplendence of that uselessness which can never be included in any reckoning.'[14]

Because it evades the propositional form, it is not easy to mark the *there* linguistically. It can be found neither in thinking nor in intuition. Goosebumps [*Gänsehaut*] come closer to it than the retina [*Netzhaut*]. It is disclosed at the pre-reflexive level. To begin with, being-*there* finds expression as being-*in-a-mood* [*Gestimmt*-Sein], which precedes the being of *consciousness* [*Bewusst*-Sein]. Mood [*Stimmung*] is not a subjective state that rubs off on the objective world. It *is* the world. Mood is even more objective than objects, without, however, being an object itself.

35

Before I direct my attention at an object, *I* already *find myself* in a *mooded* world [be-*stimmten* Welt]. Mood is a condition that precedes any object-related intentionality: 'The mood has already disclosed, in every case, Being-in-the-world as a whole, and makes it possible first of all to direct oneself towards something.'[15] Mood discloses to us the space in which we encounter beings. Mood reveals being.

Mood is not at our disposal. It takes hold of us. It is impossible to bring it about intentionally. Rather, we are thrown into it. What initially determines our being-in-the-world is not activity but thrownness: primordial ontological passivity. In the form of mood, the world reveals itself in its unavailability. Mood precedes any activity, and at the same time is de-*termining* (be-s*timmend*) for activities. Without us being aware of it, every action is a de-*termined* action. A mood thus represents the *pre-reflexive context* for activity and action. It can favour or prevent certain [be-*stimmte*] actions. A passivity dwells at the innermost core of activity. Actions and activities are accordingly not entirely free or spontaneous.

Nor is thinking pure activity or spontaneity. The contemplative dimension of thinking makes it a *correspondence*. It corresponds to what 'appeals to us as the voice of being' by letting itself be de-*termined* [be-*stimmen*] by that voice.[16] To think means to 'open our ears', that is, to listen, to lend an ear.[17] Speaking presupposes listening and correspondence:

> *Philosophia* is the expressly established correspondence which speaks in so far as it considers the appeal of the Being of being. The correspondence listens to the voice

of the appeal. Correspondence is necessary and always attuned, and not just accidentally and occasionally. It is in an attunement. And only on the basis of the attunement (disposition) does the language of correspondence obtain its precision, its tuning.[18]

A mood is nothing undetermined or vague. Rather, it gives what is thought its de-*termination* [Be-*Stimmtheit*]. A mood is a centre of gravity that condenses words and concepts into a de-*termined* thinking. It gives thinking a de-*termined* direction at the pre-reflexive level. Without mood, thinking is without destination, that is, without de-*termination* [Be-*Stimmung*]. It becomes entirely unde-*termined* [unbe-*stimmt*] and arbitrary: 'If the basic mood is lacking, then everything is a forced clatter of concepts and of the mere shells of words.'[19]

Thinking is always already *attuned*, that is, exposed to a mood that *grounds* it. The pre-reflexive grounding of thinking precedes all individual thought: 'All essential thinking demands that its thoughts and utterances be newly extracted each time, like an ore, out of the basic mood.'[20] Heidegger attempts to excavate the level of passivity in thinking. His assumption is that, in its innermost core, thinking is a *pathos*: '*pathos* is connected with *paschein*, to suffer, endure, undergo, to be borne along by, to be determined by'.[21]

Because it is not capable of pathos, artificial intelligence is not capable of thinking. Suffering and enduring are conditions that no machine can realize. Contemplative inactivity, in particular, is alien to the machine. It knows only two states: on and off. Simply deactivating the machine does not bring about a contemplative state.

In fact, a machine is neither active nor inactive. Activity and inactivity relate to one another like light and shadow. The shadow gives the light its form, its contours. Shadow and light condition each other. Similarly, activity and inactivity can be understood as two different states or modes of thinking, even of spirit. Thinking weaves itself out of light and shadow. Machine intelligence, by contrast, knows neither light nor shadow. It is *transparent*.

Contemplation is opposed to production. Contemplation engages with what is unavailable yet *already given*. *Thinking is always in the mode of reception*. The dimension of the gift in thinking makes thinking a thanking. In thinking as thanking, the will abdicates completely:

> *Guide*: And forbearing noble-mindedness [*der langmütige Edelmut*] would be a pure resting-in-itself of that willing which, renouncing willing, has let itself engage in what is not a will.
>
> *Scholar*: Noble-mindedness would be the essence of thinking and thus of thanking.[22]

Heidegger's 'reflection' resists the universal availability that makes everything accessible, calculable, controllable, steerable, manageable and consumable. With digitalization, availability reaches new heights. By bringing about total *producibility*, digitalization suspends facticity itself. The digital regime does not acknowledge an unavailable ground of being. Its motto is: *being is information*. Information makes being fully available. When everything is readily available and consumable, contemplative attention is impossible. Like a hunter, the gaze screens its surroundings. We thereby lose the *towering opposite* [*ragende Gegenüber*], where we could *linger*. Everything is smoothed out and made to serve short-term needs.

Heidegger's vocabulary of inactivity also includes 'renunciation'. This concept does not refer to a giving up or letting go of everything. Like other tropes of inactivity, it founds a constructive relation to the sphere of being that remains closed to activities controlled by the will. Renunciation is a *passion for the non-available*. In renouncing, we become able to perceive the gift: 'Renunciation does not take away, it gives.'[23] Thus renunciation turns into 'gratitude'.

Heidegger even identifies a dimension of inactivity in capacity [*Vermögen*], something we usually associate with activity and performance. He conceives of capacity from the perspective of 'liking' [*Mögen*] and 'loving':

> To embrace a 'thing' or a 'person' in their essence means to love them, to favour them. Thought in a more original way such favoring means the bestowal of their essence as a gift. Such favoring [*Mögen*] is the proper essence of enabling [*Vermögen*], which not only can achieve this or that but also can let something essentially unfold in its provenance, that is, let it be.[24]

Capacity [*Vermögen*] liberates a person or a thing into their essence by liking [*mögen*] them. Instead of taking human actions as absolutely fundamental, capacity, which does *not act*, draws on the *possible*. The word 'possible' [*möglich*] is derived from 'liking' [*mögen*]. What is possible is what is likeable. As a liking, capacity leaves the possible, the likeable, in its essence, rather than exposing it to the impossible. The rescue of the earth depends on this *ethics of inactivity*:

> Mortals dwell in that they save [*retten*] the earth – taking the word in the old sense still known to Lessing. Saving does not only snatch something from a danger. To save really means to set something free into its own presencing.[25]

Given the scale of the natural disasters we face, 'environmental protection' is an insufficient concept. What we need is a radically transformed relationship to nature. The earth is not a 'resource' that we must now 'preserve'. Rather, we must internalize the original meaning of 'preserving' [*schonen*]. Again, Heidegger interprets this term from the perspective of inactivity and of letting-be:

> Real sparing [*Schonen*] . . . takes place when we leave something beforehand in its own essence, when we retain it specifically in its presencing . . . *The fundamental character of dwelling is this sparing and preserving.*[26]

The word *schonen*, to spare or preserve, is derived from 'beautiful' [*schön*]. Sparing and preserving is directed at the beautiful. The earth is beautiful. It presents us with the imperative to spare and preserve it, to return to it its dignity.

There can be no doubt that the determination to act is necessary in order to rectify the catastrophic consequences of human intervention in nature. But if the cause of the impending disaster is the view that what is absolutely fundamental is human action – action that has ruthlessly appropriated and exploited nature – then we require a corrective to human action itself. We must therefore increase *the proportion of action that is contemplative*, that is, ensure that action is enriched *by reflection*.

The compulsion to be active, to produce and to perform, leads to breathlessness. Under the weight of their own doings, humans suffocate. It is only in the state of reflection that 'things become spacious, airy around the human being'.[27] Heidegger's *Black Notebooks* contain a very noteworthy remark: 'Beyng is the aether in which mankind breathes; without this aether humans would descend to the level of mere beasts and even lower, and all human activity would be reduced to breeding like cattle.'[28] What Heidegger suggests here is a *biopolitics based on the history of being*. Forgetfulness of being, resulting from the lack of reflection, takes our breath away. It reduces the human being to an *animal laborans*. From this perspective, inactivity has political significance. A politics of reflection would need to counteract those compulsions that mould human beings into farm animals.

Like Hannah Arendt, the early Heidegger was animated by the *pathos* of action. Contemplative inactivity was still utterly alien to him. Although he discovered the 'thrownness' of human existence, thrownness is outshone by the 'resoluteness' of action. He even interprets moods such as 'anxiety' and 'boredom', which may in fact inhibit action, as calls to act. The so-called 'turn', in which he moved away from his earlier thought, marks the *transition from acting to being*.

In *Being and Time*, anxiety represents the 'basic state-of-mind' because it confronts *Dasein* (Heidegger's ontological term for the human being) with its Being-in-the-world.[29] Unlike fear, which relates only to *something* in the world, the object of anxiety is the *world as such*: 'That which anxiety is anxious about is Being-in-the-world itself. In anxiety . . . entities within-the-world [sink away]. The "world" can offer nothing more, and neither can the Dasein-with of Others.'[30] This world, which slips away from anxious Dasein, is not the world as such, but the familiar, everyday world in which we carry on with our lives unquestioningly. It is dominated by the 'they' [*man*], by the conformism of 'publicly interpreted things':

We take pleasure and enjoy ourselves as *they* [*man*] take pleasure; we read, see, and judge . . . as *they* see and judge . . . The 'they', which is nothing definite, and which all are, though not as the sum, prescribes the kind of Being of everydayness.[31]

The 'they', as the no one, relieves Dasein of the burden of the responsibility to decide by unburdening it of the need to *act* in the genuine sense. The 'they' provides Dasein with a prefabricated world in which everything has already been interpreted and decided. Everydayness, the intellectual and behavioural patterns unthinkingly accepted by everyone, is a construction of the 'they'. It prevents Dasein from being *someone* who – in acting – explicitly takes responsibility for his own self. The 'they' undermines any independent perspective on the world. Heidegger calls this mode of being 'inauthenticity' or 'fallenness'. First and foremost – and most of the time – Dasein exists inauthentically. It closes itself off from the possibility of being properly itself. It is only anxiety that enables Dasein to be itself, that is, to *act*. With this step of the argument, Heidegger expects anxiety to be something that, strictly speaking, it cannot be, for anxiety means precisely the *impossibility* of action. Heidegger, however, takes anxiety to be the *possibility* of taking hold of one's proper self and deciding to act.

For Heidegger, boredom is not the dream bird that hatches the egg of experience. Rather, he interprets boredom, too, as a call to act. In the state of boredom, just as in the state of anxiety, the world – that is, beings in their totality – slips away from Dasein. Dasein ends up in paralyzing emptiness. All 'possibilities of doing and acting' fail. But in this failure [*Versagen*] Heidegger hears a telling [*ein Sagen*]: 'What do beings in this telling refusal of themselves as a whole tell us in such refusal? ... The very possibilities of its [i.e. Dasein's] doing and acting.'[32] The refusal is at the same time the '*telling announcement* [*Ansagen*] *of possibilities left unexploited*', which the human being has to seize with heroic determination [*Entschlossenheit*].[33] Boredom makes an urgent appeal on behalf of 'acting here and now'. This disclosure [*Sichentschließen*] of one's proper self, that is, the decision to be someone, is the '*moment of vision*'.[34]

Being and Time is dominated by an emphasis on the self and on action. Even death is understood in terms of the ability to be oneself. In the face of death, the 'uttermost possibility' of 'giving itself up', Dasein awakens to a forceful *I-am*.[35] Death, *my* death, entails an emphasis on the self. Death leads to a consolidation of the self. Heidegger could not imagine the experience of death in terms of a loosening of the grip of the self. That kind of death would mean that, in the face of death, I deal death

43

to myself, rather than holding on to my ego. By opening up the *other* for me, it would liberate me, awakening a *releasement* [*Gelassenheit*], a *friendliness towards the world*.[36]

The emphasis on the self is accompanied by a determination to act. The emphasis on the self is itself a *form of activity*. There is no such determined self under the condition of inactivity. The master of inactivity does not say 'I'. *Being and Time* has no space for inactivity. The world is everywhere a 'work-world'.[37] Things are tools. Everything is subordinated to the in-order-to. The fundamental condition of human existence is 'care'. There is no *festive space* that transcends 'everydayness'. *Being and Time* finds no place for festivities and games, where 'care' is fully suspended.

A few years after the publication of *Being and Time*, Heidegger's thought underwent a transition from acting to being. The *pathos* of acting gives way to a *wonder about the world*:

> For celebrating, as a pausing from work, is indeed already a keeping to oneself; it is a taking note, a questioning, a reflecting, an awaiting, passing over into the more wakeful intimation of wonder, namely, of the wonder that a world worlds around us at all, that beings are and not rather nothing, that things are and that we ourselves in their midst are.[38]

The emphasis on the self and action that dominates *Being and Time* falls completely silent. Anxiety and boredom are no longer tied to an appeal to act. They reveal *Being*. In this, they resemble love:

> Profound boredom . . . removes all things and human

beings and oneself along with them into a remarkable indifference. This boredom manifests beings as a whole.

Another possibility of such manifestation is concealed in our joy in the presence of the Dasein – and not simply of the person – of a human being whom we love.[39]

Following the 'turn', Heidegger realizes that human existence gets its radiance only from inactivities, such as festivals and play. He discovers the dimension of the festive; he no longer talks about 'care' or 'anxiety'. The grey of everyday reality gives way to festive radiance:

To the festive there belongs radiance. Radiance, however, properly arises from the illumination and shining of the essential. Insofar as the essential radiates, every aspect of things and humans enters into the release of its radiance, and this radiance in turn demands of human beings adornment and ornamentation. . . . To the radiance of celebration belong play and dance.[40]

Play and dance are entirely free of the in-order-to. Even ornaments do not serve the purpose of adorning something; they are not a 'ware' [Zeug]. Things, liberated from the in-order-to, become festive. They do not 'function' but shine and radiate. They emanate a contemplative calmness that enables a lingering.

The festival, the radiant form of human existence, dispels the cramped rigidity of the Dasein that resolves to act. The festival liberates human existence from the narrowness of aims and actions, from the yoke of purpose and usefulness. In the festival mood, the cramped time of 'care', the existential tension that has its source in the self, is suspended. The emphasis on the self gives way to releasement [*Gelassenheit*] and exuberance [*Ausgelassenheit*]. Contemplative lingering replaces the *pathos* of action.

Heidegger's thinking contains *traces* that we might condense into an *ethics of inactivity*. Such an ethics would concern our relationship towards nature as well as relationships between human beings. A few years before his death, Heidegger wrote a short text titled 'Andenken an Marcelle Mathieu' [In memory of Marcelle Mathieu]. Its subject is the hospitality of Heidegger's then recently deceased hostess in Provence. Heidegger begins by invoking the vast landscape of her homeland, as if her hospitality was a direct result of her intense relationship with it. He emphasizes the timidity she felt in relation to the landscape: 'The inconspicuousness [*Unscheinbare*] of her timidity [*Scheu*] began to shine only when the lady of Les Camphoux invited friends to the Le Rebanqué hill, with its rich, all-encompassing views over the vast landscape.'[41] The vast landscape fills the hostess with a wonderment and awe that causes her *to take herself back, disarm herself, and clear her inner self*. Her timidity in the face of the landscape expands into her interpersonal relations, and finds its expression in the form of hospitality.

The *towering other* of the vast landscape elicits timidity in the observer, who confronts the unavailable. Heidegger speaks of the 'hesitant awe in the face of what cannot be made'.[42] Whoever is awe-struck in this way delivers *himself* to the *other of the self*. In awe, a special kind of attention arises, a *friendly receptivity* for the other. Awe teaches us to *listen*. It makes the hostess an attentive listener: 'During the conversations between the friends, she remained a quietly attentive listener, caring only about their well-being. In these moments, she was neither dame nor maid but, holding back from both, subservient to something unspoken. It was probably this unspoken with which she was in quiet dialogue on her many long, solitary hiking tours through her homeland.'[43] In this passage, Heidegger derives the ability to listen from the power of the 'unspoken' that is expressed in the vast landscape. Heidegger's hostess listens *herself* away by letting herself be at-*tuned* [be-*stimmen*] by the 'unspoken'. The 'unspoken' is the *language of the earth* that escapes the human will. The fate of the earth depends on our ability *to listen to the earth*.

In *Country Path Conversations*, Heidegger remarks on the character of a 'guest': 'He can listen, and indeed do so with such courteous anticipation that, for me, because of this prevailing gesture and attitude of his, he is the guest *par excellence*.'[44] Confronted with the vastness of the landscape, Heidegger's hostess feels herself a guest. She is *a guest between earth and sky*. She is 'neither dame nor maid'. As a guest, she obeys the 'unspoken', by listening to it. *Her timidity sharpens her attentiveness.*

The behaviour of Heidegger's hostess expresses his *ethics of timidity*. Heidegger conveys this in the following anecdote: 'And the shyness? She left a precious trace of it for us here in Freiburg, when, on a planned visit, standing in front of our house, she did not dare to ring the bell – and left again. In this way, what is not done is sometimes more powerful than what is said and done.'[45] Heidegger could also have said: not-doing is more powerful than anything done or achieved. *The ethics of timidity is the ethics of inactivity.*

Absolute Lack of Being

The root of the current crisis is the disintegration of everything that gives life meaning and orientation. Life is no longer *borne* by anything that supports it, and that we can support. The crisis is best expressed in a line from Rilke's *Duino Elegies*: 'For nowhere is there a staying.'[1] Never has life been so fleeting, transient, mortal.

'Immortality', Hannah Arendt remarks, 'has fled the world to find an uncertain abode in the darkness of the human heart that still has the capacity to remember and to say: forever.' Imperishability 'has taken its homeless refuge in the very heart of mortality', namely the mortal human being.[2] In this context, Arendt quotes Rilke:

The mountains rest, shone over by the stars –
but even in them time glimmers.

48

Ah, in my wild heart for the night,
homeless, the imperishable lies.[3]

In fact, Rilke's poem laments the incessant diminution of *being*. The first verse runs:

Odd, the words: 'while away the time'.
How to *hold it fast* the harder thing.
Who is not fearful: where is there a staying,
where in all this is there any *being*?[4]

Today, the human heart is incapable of offering refuge to the imperishable. The heart is the organ of remembrance and memory, and in the digital age we are without heart. We store vast quantities of data and information without, however, indulging in remembrance. We turn away from any kind of 'forever'. We renounce time-intensive practices such as faithfulness, responsibility, promising, trust and commitment. The provisional, the short term and the impermanent dominate our lives.

Time increasingly disintegrates and becomes a mere succession of point-like presences. It becomes additive. There is no narrative to give it *structure*, to make it stand still. Temporal architectures erode. Rituals and festivals are temporal architectures that give the passage of time a skeletal structure, so to speak, and in this way stabilize it. Such temporal architectures obstruct the circulation of information and capital, and are therefore dismantled.

The digitalization and informatization of the world fragment time and make life radically transient. *Being* has a temporal aspect. It grows slowly and gradually. Today's short-termism dismantles being. Being forms only under

49

conditions of lingering. Information represents the *highest point of being's atrophy*. Niklas Luhmann said of information: 'Its cosmology is a cosmology not of being but of contingency.'[5] Being disintegrates into information. We register information only fleetingly. After that, its status as being moves towards nil, like answerphone messages once we have listened to them. Information is topical only briefly. Its appeal is its capacity to surprise, and its effect is to produce in us a frenzy of topicality.

The human being is an *animal narrans*, a *narrating animal*. But our lives are no longer determined by a reliable and binding narrative that provides meaning and orientation. We are very well informed, yet, in the absence of narrative, we are without orientation. If human happiness, as Nietzsche says, depends on there being an '*incontrovertible* truth', we are indeed without happiness.[6] Truth is a narrative. Information, by contrast, is additive. It does not congeal into a narrative. It intensifies the *digital storm of contingency* and aggravates the absence of being. Nothing promises commitment or duration. The intensification of contingency destabilizes life.

Today's world lacks symbols that stabilize temporal axes. Symbolic perception, that is, *recognition*, sees the *lasting*. *Repetition* deepens being. Symbolic perception is free from contingency; it is not the serial perception that registers one bit of information after another. Data and information have no symbolic power.

The symbolic has an immediate effect on perception. It influences our behaviour and thinking at the pre-reflexive, emotional, aesthetic level. Symbols create *shared things* that enable a *We*: cohesion within society. *Shared feeling*, the *sym-pathos* or *com-passion*, comes about

50

only with the symbolic and aesthetic. In a symbolic void, society is diffracted into a collection of mutually indifferent individuals, for what unites and creates commitment no longer exists. The loss of common feeling grounded in the symbolic intensifies the lack of being. A community is a symbolically mediated totality. The symbolic-narrative void therefore leads to the fragmentation and erosion of society.

Plato's dialogue *Symposium* tells us what a symbol actually is. Aristophanes says that human beings were originally completely round. Because they became too powerful and arrogant, the gods cut them in half. Since then, each half has sought to re-unite with its other half. In Greek, such a fragment is called *symbolon*. As a *symbolon*, the human being longs for a wholesome, healing totality. This longing is love. The restored totality would heal the wound, remove the lack of being caused by the original split:

> In the case of the symbol ... and for our experience of the symbolic in general, the particular represents itself as a fragment of being that promises to complete and make whole whatever corresponds to it. Or, indeed, the symbol is that other fragment that has always been sought in order to complete and make whole our own fragmentary life.[7]

The symbolic promises a fullness of being, a salvation. Without a symbolic order, we remain splinters and fragments.

We use most of our powers to extend life. In so doing, we succeed only in reducing life to survival. *We live in order to survive.* The mania for health and optimization is a reflexive response to the lack of being. We try to compensate for the absence of being by extending bare life, and in so doing we become desensitized to *life's intensity*. We confuse it with increased production, performance and consumption, but these are merely *forms of survival*.

The lack of being is also caused by economic processes that increasingly isolate people from each other. Because being is *being-with*, isolation and loneliness lead to a lack of being. No *we* can come about in the neoliberal performance society. The neoliberal regime increases productivity by isolating people and forcing them to compete. It transforms life into a battle for survival, into a hell of unbridled competition. Success, performance and competition are forms of survival.

Digitalization is another factor that undermines being as being-with. Being connected is not the same as being together. In fact, unlimited connectivity weakens our ties. A deep relationship requires an *other* who can make themselves unavailable. With digitalization, however, the *Thou* becomes an *It*, which creates a *fundamental loneliness*. A consumable object that satisfies our needs is not something with which we can form a proper tie. Despite the growth of digital connectivity, then, we are lonelier than ever before.

A real tie forms when we invest an object with libidinal energy. But without proper ties, there is a reflux of this psychic energy; it streams back into the self. This psychic reflux, the congested libidinal energy that is not invested in the other, makes us anxious. Anxiety results from a lack of object attachment. The self, thrown back on itself, begins to circle around itself in a worldless movement. The absent Eros intensifies the lack of being. Only Eros can defeat anxiety and depression.

The lack of being causes an excess of production. Today's hyperactivity and hyper-communication can be interpreted as a reaction to a lack of being. The lack of being is fought with material growth. We *produce against* the feeling of lack. The zenith of productivity probably comes as *being* reaches its nadir. Capital is a form of survival. Capitalism is nurtured by the illusion that more capital creates more life, increases the capacity to live. But this life is a *bare* life, a survival.

A feeling of lack impels us to act. Someone who is determined to act does not look out. By contrast, someone who exclaims, with Faust, 'Bide here, you are so beautiful', will not act. Fullness of being, that is, *beauty*, is found in the contemplative gaze. We have completely forgotten that the highest happiness is owed to contemplation. In antiquity, as well as in the Middle Ages, happiness was sought in contemplation. The Greek poet Menander wrote:

> I maintain, Parmenon, that the happiest man is the one who, after happily viewing [ohne Leid *geschaut*] these impressive phenomena – the sun which is there for all, the stars, the rain, the clouds and the lightning – soon returns to the place from which he came. Whether you live to be a hundred, or have a short life, you will never see these things change, and you will never see anything more impressive.[8]

Asked 'for what end he had been born', the Greek philosopher Anaxagoras answered: for 'contemplation' [*Zum*

Schauen] (*eis theorian*).[9] When we are born, we are released from the objectless darkness into the bright world. The newborn open their eyes not to act but to look. *Natality* is founded on looking, not on acting, on the wonder at what there *is*, not on the pathos of the new. Being born means seeing the light of the world. For Homer, life is identical with 'the light of heaven to view'.[10]

Of course, the active life has its own validity and justification. However, its ultimate purpose is, according to Aquinas, to serve the *vita contemplativa*: 'vita contemplativa est dispositio ad contemplativam'.[11] The *vita contemplativa* is 'the end of the whole human life' (*finis totius humanae vitae*).[12] The contemplative gaze is our whole reward for our effort: '*tota merces nostra visio est*'.[13] And a work, the result of activity, is complete only when it offers itself up to our vision.

In his commentary on the *Nicomachean Ethics*, Aquinas offers a highly idiosyncratic definition of politics. He formulates a *politics of inactivity* that is the opposite of Arendt's understanding of politics. Politics misses its goal if it does not open itself up to the non-political. Its ultimate purpose is inactivity, contemplation: 'This is contemplative happiness, to which the whole of political life seems directed; as long as the arrangement of political life establishes and preserves peace, it gives men the opportunity of contemplating truth.'[14]

In the face of perfect being, which lacks nothing, one can only ever *look* and *praise*. Augustine's *De civitate Dei* (*The City of God*) thus ends with a panegyric on the divine fullness of being. The Sabbath promises the kingdom of God, 'of which there is no end'. And what shall we do in the eternal kingdom of God? – 'There we shall rest in eternity [*in aeterno*] and see, see [*videbimus, videbimus*] and love, love [*amabimus, amabimus*] and praise [*laudabimus*].' 'Behold', Augustine continues, 'what will be in the end to which there shall be no end.'[15] In Augustine, seeing and loving become one. Only where there is love do the eyes open (*ubi amor, ibi oculus*).[16] Seeing and praising are kinds of inactivity. They do not pursue any purpose; they do not produce anything. The lack of being is all that keeps the machine of production going.

The ultimate purpose of language is praise. Praise gives language a festive radiance. Praise restores being; it sings about and invokes the fullness of being. In one of his poems, Rilke makes praise the task of the poet: 'O tell us poet, what it is you do? – I praise.'[17] In the poet's praise, language enters a festive and contemplative calmness. Praise is the *Sabbath of language*. It expresses the *being* finite [endlich *Sein*] that radiates throughout the mortal human heart:[18]

> To praise, that's it! Called to praise,
> he came like ore out of the silence
> of stone. Oh, his heart's a perishable press
> of a wine that's eternal for men.
>
> When he's in a godlike example's grip,
> his voice isn't graveled by drought.
> All turns vineyard, all turns grape,
> ripened in his sensitive South.[19]

Rilke distinguishes praising from 'wooing': 'No more wooing! Voice, you've outgrown wooing.'[20] Wooing necessarily involves a lack; it is a part of the 'anxious creature' [*kümmerndes Tier*]²¹ whose essential trait is *care*. Praise, by contrast, has *outgrown* all striving, all care. In this lies its festive nature. Where there is an absence of being, there is no praise. There is only the *bustle of commercial wooing*. All communication today is advertising as a form of survival. This form of survival is triggered at the *zero point of being*.

Festive time is a time of intensified attention [*gesteigertes Schauen*]. The 'festive feeling' is an intensified feeling of being.²² Festivals brighten the world by providing meaning and orientation:

> The festival reveals the meaning of everyday existence, the essence of the things that surround the human being, and of the forces that are active in its own nature. The festival, as a reality in the world of humans ... means that, at rhythmically returning intervals, mankind is able to become *contemplative* [*beschaulich*], and in this condition directly faces the higher realities on which its whole existence rests.²³

The time of the festival, which we *enter* [*begehen*] as we would enter a room that is decorated for a festival, does not *pass* [*vergeht nicht*]. It is an exalted time [*Hoch-Zeit*].²⁴ The festival brings forth a timelessness in which the lack of being vanishes.

Work separates and isolates people. The absolute value given to work and performance dismantles being as a being-with. The festival, by contrast, founds community. It gathers and binds people together. The festive feeling is always a *feeling of community*, a *we-feeling*. For Hans-Georg Gadamer, the festival is the foundation of

56

community: 'A festival is an experience of community and represents community in its most perfect form.'[25]

When looking [*Schauen*] was human beings' primary relationship to the world, they still had a relationship to the fullness of divine being. The Greek word *theoria* (to look) derives from *theoroi*, an envoy who travelled to a distant place to attend a festival celebrating the gods. To observe the divine is *theoria*. *Theoroi* are the spirit seers of the gods. Looking intensified by the festive turns the spectator into a *theoroi*: 'When Aeschylus called the spectator *theoros* rather than *theates*, what he had in mind was an expanded form of looking that was festive also in its enormity.'[26] To the extent that they have knowledge of the divine, philosophers are also *theoroi*. The scholar Harpocration of Alexandria describes *theoroi* thus: 'Moreover, not only are the spectators called *theoroi*, but they also used to so name those sent to gods and in general those who keep the sacred things or see to the sacred things.'[27] When Aristotle gives the *bios theoretikos*, that is, contemplative life, the status of a divine activity, he clearly has in mind the cultic vision of God (*theoptia*):

And then, finally, there is Aristotle who compares the philosophers' *theoria* not with any arbitrary seeing [*Schau*] but with the event at Olympia, to which *theoriai* were actually sent, and with the Dionysian festivals. Independent of any relations with ritual practices he finds the divine in this seeing.[28]

The human being is able to lead a *bios theoretikos* 'in so far as something divine is present in him'.[29] Aristotle strongly emphasizes that the gods do not act:

We assume the gods to be above all other beings blessed and happy; but what sort of actions must we assign to them? Acts of justice? Will not the gods seem absurd if they make contracts and return deposits, and so on? Acts of a brave man, then, confronting dangers and running risks because it is noble to do so? Or liberal acts? To whom will they give? It will be strange if they are really to have money or anything of the kind. And what would their temperate acts be? Is not such praise tasteless, since they have no bad appetites? If we were to run through them all, the circumstances of action would be found trivial and unworthy of gods. Still, everyone supposes that they *live* and therefore that they are active; we cannot suppose them to sleep like Endymion. Now if you take away from a living being action, and still more production, what is left but contemplation?[30]

The activity of the God, 'which surpasses all others in blessedness', is contemplative activity (*theoretike*).[31] The activity of contemplation is an inactivity, a contemplative calmness, leisure (*schole*) to the extent that, unlike active life (*bios politikos*), it does not *act*; that is, it does not have its purpose outside of itself. In its inactivity, its leisure, life relates to itself. Life is no longer estranged from itself. Aristotle therefore associates *bios theoretikos* with self-sufficiency: 'And the self-sufficiency that is spoken of must belong most to the contemplative activity.'[32] Only *vita contemplativa* promises divine self-sufficiency and perfect blessedness.

History is complete when action gives way to contemplation, that is, when the *Sabbath of inactivity* arrives. The sight of a person regarding a work of art in rapt contemplation led the philosopher George Santayana to formulate a decisive philosophical insight: 'how instrumental were all the labor and history of man, to be crowned, if crowned at all, only in intuition'.[33]

The *Pathos* of Action

There are two divine (*qadosch*) concepts in Judaism: God and Sabbath. God is Sabbath. For a devout Jew, life is nothing but a 'striving for Sabbath'.[1] Sabbath means salvation. On the Sabbath, the human being is immortal. The passage of time is suspended. The Sabbath is a 'palace in time' that releases the human being from the transient world into the world to come (*Olam Haba*).[2] *Menucha* (rest) is a synonym for the world to come. The deep sense of the Sabbath is the suspension of history in blissful inactivity.

The creation of man is not the last act of Genesis. It is only with the Sabbath that creation is truly complete. In his commentary on Genesis, Rashi writes: 'What was the world lacking? Rest. The Sabbath came, and so came rest. The work was completed and finished.'[3] The rest on the Sabbath does not simply come after the work of creation; rather, it completes it. The world that is created in six days is the nuptial chamber, so to speak, but it lacks the bride. Only with the Sabbath does the bride arrive.[4] The Sabbath festival is an exalted time [*Hoch-Zeit*], a time that stands still. The Sabbath is not the day on which God rests to recover from the tiring work of creation. Rather, rest is the essence of creation. Only the Sabbath gives creation divine blessing. Rest and inactivity are divine. Without rest, the human being loses the divine.

In her essay 'The Meaning of Revolution', Hannah Arendt approvingly quotes John Adams, whom she admired: 'it is action, not rest, that constitutes our pleasure'.[5] Arendt was a Jewish thinker, but her thought lacks the dimension of the Sabbath. She was inspired by the messianism of freedom and action. According to Arendt, creation is completed not with the Sabbath but with the advent of human freedom. What is divine is not Sabbath rest but freedom, that is, the 'principle of beginning':

'that there be a beginning, man was created before whom there was nobody', said Augustine in his political philosophy. This beginning is not the same as the beginning of the world; it is not the beginning of something but of somebody, who is a beginner himself. With the creation of man, the principle of beginning came into the world itself, which, of course, is only another way of saying that the principle of freedom was created when man was created but not before.[6]

According to Arendt, before man was created there was not nothing but 'nobody'. A human being is a 'somebody' to the extent that he or she acts, that is, introduces a new beginning into the world.

Arendt also eliminates the contemplative dimension in her discussion of the Greek world. As we know, the Greek *polis* consists of three spaces: *oikos*, *agora* and *temenos*. Arendt ignores the *temenos*, the sphere of religious contemplation, altogether. The political sphere becomes the *polis* as such, and it is juxtaposed with the *oikos*, the sphere of the house, household and family, in which Arendt places everything to do with the needs and necessities of pure life. Human beings are free only when they leave the house and enter the political sphere. Arendt idealizes the Greek *polis* as a utopia of the political, a noble sphere of freedom. It is the space of the 'somebody' who strives for fame and recognition, even immortality, who is inspired by the drive to be the *best* and achieve the 'extraordinary': 'The *polis* was supposed to multiply the occasions to win "immortal fame," that is, to multiply the chances for everybody to distinguish himself, to show in deed and word who he was in his unique distinctness.'[7] Arendt's conception of the *polis* is based on a need to find salvation. The *polis* is supposed to ensure that the 'most futile of human activities, action and speech . . . become imperishable'.[8] The *polis* is an 'everlasting stage' on which there exist 'only appearances but no exits'.[9] Human beings achieve immortality only through political action. The striving for immortal fame is what moves history.

According to Arendt, only a 'somebody' who displays his uniqueness before an audience can claim reality for himself. People who do not act enjoy only an animalistic 'feeling of life'. Life apart from the political stage is animal life. It lacks the 'feeling of reality':

62

To be deprived of it [the space where I appear to others as others appear to me; D.S.] means to be deprived of reality, which, humanly and politically speaking, is the same as appearance. To men the reality of the world is guaranteed by the presence of others, by its appearing to all.[10]

To be alive and to act become one and the same. Arendt's understanding of life has no place for the *contemplative life* that does not require a 'stage' or 'appearance' but is nevertheless something quite different from animal life. The *feeling for being* is supplanted by the 'feeling for reality', which is owed entirely to action, that is, to being active, to having an effect. The *festive feeling* that allows us to glimpse a higher reality is alien to Arendt.

Arendt expels the *temenos* from the Greek *polis*. A *temenos* is a sacred space that is separate from the public space and is reserved for the gods; it is a *peribolos* (literally 'hedge' or 'circumference'), that is, a fenced-in space, a delineated temple area surrounded by walls. *Temenos* is a *templum*, a consecrated, holy place, a temple, a place of contemplative vision. The word 'contemplation' is derived from *templum*. In a philosophical sense, the *temenos* is the realm of eternal ideas: 'This cut-out space houses the ideas. They are spaceless and timeless. It is possible to perceive them when looking with the theoretical gaze.'[11]

The *temenos* sits enthroned above the *polis*. It can therefore often be found situated on a hill. The Greek *polis* is inconceivable without this *Acro-polis* (literally 'high city' or 'upper city'). The Acropolis is dedicated to the divine: 'The rules that apply inside this space are different from those outside. What happens here is explicitly done in the face of the godhead, and what is located here is and remains in the possession of the godhead.'[12] The Acropolis is not a 'stage' for a 'someone'. The *pathos* of action does not fit into the *temenos*. In any case, ritual action means human beings merge into a collective body, in which context the individuality of a 'someone' is impossible. In the *temenos*, it is the gods who appear, and it is the gods who are in charge.

Sojourning in Greece, Heidegger wrote of the Acropolis: 'This *polis* did not really know subjectivity as the measure of all objectivity. It fitted the fittingness of the gods, who, in turn, were subjected to destiny, Moira.'[13] Arendt reinvents the *polis* by presenting it as the stage of the 'someone', the scene of freedom and action, completely ignoring the ritual dimension of the *polis*. There are no divine festivals in Arendt's *polis*. Festivals, rituals and games have no place in her thought, which is dominated by the *pathos* of action.

Arendt idealizes the Greek *polis*, calling it the 'most individualistic and least conformable body politic known to us'.[14] What actually happened in this sanctified political space, however, remains a mystery, and there is no substantial characterization of the *polis* as political utopia. Arendt's disciple Judith N. Shklar remarks:

Arendt's own political dream remained tied to the *polis*. In spite of what Aristotle tells us, she was never very clear about what went on in that blessed 'public space'. In fact, we know that there was ferocious fighting between rich and poor and over who would conduct the next interpolis war, and in what manner.[15]

The *polis* always addressed the 'social questions' that Arendt wanted to banish to the sphere of necessity, of mere life. Plato's *Apology* also deals a blow to Arendt's vision of the *polis*:

> Be sure, men of Athens, that if I had long ago attempted to take part in politics [*politiká prágmata*], I should have died long ago . . . Do not be angry with me for speaking the truth; no man will survive who genuinely opposes you or any other crowd and prevents the occurrence of many unjust and illegal happenings in the city.[16]

In the *polis*, speaking freely and speaking the truth (*parrhesia*) are dangerous. The person who nobly speaks the truth in opposition to the will of the masses risks his life.

Arendt's thought is nourished by political utopia. The political – where Arendt locates human freedom – is the redeeming light, the 'brightness of the human', that dissolves the 'darkness of the creaturely', the darkness of mere life.[17] For Arendt, it is clear: *being* is creaturely. *Action* is truly human. To the political Arendt assigns an ontological, even soteriological, dignity. She elevates the *polis* to the 'fenced-in space of men's free deeds and living words, which could endow life with splendour'.[18]

The *polis* is a 'fenced-in' space of freedom. The original English edition does not have the expression 'fenced-in'. Arendt added the word when she translated her text into German. The *agora*, a public space, was actually open; it was only the *temenos* that was fenced in. Subconsciously, Arendt turns the Greek *polis* into the *templum of freedom*. The expression 'fenced-in' tells us a lot about Arendt's idea of the political. She erects fences around the political to protect it against forces that would enmesh human beings in mere creaturely life, in the realm of necessity. It is only the freedom to act, which is the essential core of the political, that distinguishes human beings from 'mere living creatures', which 'live and die like animals'.[19] Human beings reach the realm of freedom when they liberate themselves from the 'necessities of sheer life' and are 'no longer bound to the biological life process'.[20] Human beings are saved from the necessities of mere life only by the freedom of action, which marks a *second birth* that elevates human beings above creaturely being: 'With word and deed we insert ourselves into the human world, a world that already existed before we were born, and this insertion is like a second birth.'[21]

Arendt's political utopia is revealed most clearly in her idea of revolution. Revolution, she believes, is the highest expression of human freedom. It is synonymous with freedom understood as a new beginning:

> What the revolutions brought to the fore was this experience of being free . . . the experience of man's faculty to begin something new. . . . Only where this pathos of novelty is present and where novelty is connected with the idea of freedom are we entitled to speak of revolution.[22]

Arendt projects her political utopia on to revolution. For this reason, her revolution does not aim at liberation from want, misery, hunger, poverty, injustice, or oppression, but at founding freedom. The expansion of inalienable civil rights to all humankind is not revolutionary. It means freedom from unjustified constraints and as such represents only a negative freedom, that is, a liberation. What is truly revolutionary is a freedom that provides access to the public sphere for everyone, for which liberation is only a necessary condition. Liberation in the sense of negative freedom does not necessarily lead to participation in public life.

Arendt's noble idea of freedom, her messianism of freedom, relegates all social issues, even the social as such, to the realm of necessity. The political is completely decoupled from the social. The social embodies mere life, and mere life prevents us from entering the realm of freedom. According to Arendt, the French Revolution failed precisely because of the social dimension. The misery of the masses represents an 'obstacle to freedom'.[23] The urgent needs of the masses and their attempts to avoid their plight are not conducive to the realization of freedom. The political is not open to people who are slaves to mere life. The appearance on the political stage of the misery of social need suffocates the budding idea of freedom:

If it were true, as all participants moved by the misery of the people suddenly agreed, that the goal of revolutions was the happiness of the people – *le but de la Révolution est le bonheur du peuple* – then indeed it could be provided by a sufficiently enlightened despotic government rather than a republic.[24]

Happiness is not a goal of politics. Happiness, like misery, belongs to the realm of necessity.

In the final analysis, Arendt's understanding of the French Revolution is non-political. In fact, however, the desperate masses strode on to the political stage as soon as they streamed into the streets of Paris and became publicly visible. The attempt to exit the state of invisibility to which they were condemned by their rulers was genuinely political. Arendt's non-political understanding of the French Revolution follows, paradoxically, from her utopian concept of the political. The masses cannot occupy the political stage, which is reserved for a 'someone' striving for immortal fame. The people are consigned to mere life.

Arendt's notion of action casts the American Revolution in a positive light. The men of the American Revolution, Arendt says, were fortunate not to have to confront the obstacle to freedom that is the social. They owed their success to the 'invisibility of slaves'.[25] The *hommes des lettres* could thus keep to themselves and realize their idea of freedom unperturbed by the misery of African Americans. For Arendt, the liberation of the slaves would not, in any case, have been a political act, for they – and this may sound cynical from today's perspective – 'were not so much constrained by political oppression as the sheer necessities of life'.[26] Arendt ignores the French Revolution's achievements in abolishing aristocracy and serfdom – genuine political acts that make the French Revolution more significant than the American.

For Arendt, social issues do not belong to politics, that noble sphere of freedom. Social issues pollute public debates like a 'plague'.[27] Such issues have to do with mere creaturely life, from which politics should distance itself. Arendt emphasizes:

It may be that ancient political theory, which held that economics, since it was bound up with the necessities

68

of life, needed the rule of masters to function well, and for that very reason should play no role in the *polis*, the realm of the political, was not so wrong after all.[28]

The redeeming light of the political sphere casts all social and economic issues into the shadows. Arendt describes Lenin's definition of the October Revolution – 'Electrification plus *soviets*' – as 'an entirely un-Marxist separation of economics and politics, a differentiation between electrification as the solution of Russia's social question, and the *soviet* system as her new body politic'. What Arendt finds 'perhaps even more surprising' – coming from a Marxist – is 'the suggestion that the problem of poverty is not to be solved through socialization and socialism, but through technical means'.[29] For her, social want and poverty are the domain of technology, not of politics. She ignores the fact that in Europe it was precisely the industrial capitalism of the eighteenth and nineteenth centuries that brought about such poverty and misery; that industrialization, when left to itself and released from political control, leads to terror.

Arendt repeatedly denies the connection between poverty and politics. It is important, she says, 'to keep in mind that poverty cannot be defeated by political means'.[30] Poverty is a purely technical affair: 'Nothing, we might say today, could be more obsolete than to attempt to liberate mankind from poverty by political means; nothing could be more futile and more dangerous.'[31] Today, there exists 'the very legitimate hope that the advancement of the natural sciences will open, in a not too distant future, possibilities of dealing with the economic matters on technical grounds outside of all political considerations'.[32]

She adds: 'every attempt to solve the social question with political means leads to terror'.[33]

For Arendt to acknowledge that the causes of slavery, hunger and misery are first and foremost political and economic, that social questions are always political in nature, that the exploited or immiserated are victims of the structural violence of global capitalism, she would need to dispense with her noble idea of the political. Jean Ziegler puts it succinctly: 'Every child who starves to death is murdered.'[34] Hunger and misery reflect global relations of domination that are murderous and violent. Arendt's political utopia is blind to the relations of power and domination that traverse economic space. Her conception of the political space as a 'stage' for a 'someone' turns out to be non-political.

Arendt's insistence on isolating the political sphere from the economic and social is a result of her *messianism of freedom*, her *soteriological urge* to create a space of freedom beyond the needs and necessities of mere life. She repeatedly invokes 'the great saving event or "miracle" which will redeem mankind time and again'.[35] Arendt's messianic hope is based on the birth of Jesus:

> It is this faith in and hope for the world that found perhaps its most glorious and most succinct expression in the few words with which the Gospels announced their 'glad tidings': 'A child has been born unto us.'[36]

The *pathos* of the new, and of new beginnings, which Arendt idealizes as the exemplification of freedom, was alien to the Greek *polis*. This *pathos* emerges instead from the spirit of the modern age. The emphasis on absolute novelty that took hold of the sciences in the modern age was also the basis of the French Revolution. Arendt herself associates the *pathos* of the new with the modern age:

> the strange pathos of novelty, so characteristic of the modern age, needed almost two hundred years to leave the relative seclusion of scientific and philosophic thought and to reach the realm of politics. . . . It was only in the course of the eighteenth-century revolutions that men began to be aware that a new beginning could be a political phenomenon, that it could be the result of what men had done and what they could consciously set out to do.[37]

Kierkegaard's elevation of 'repetition' over the new is very much a revolt against the spirit of the modern age. 'One becomes weary', he says, 'only of what is new. One never grows weary of the old.' The old 'is the daily bread that satisfies with blessing'.[38] The daily bread is not appealing. Only what has no appeal permits repetition. Repetition reveals an intensity in what does not appeal. Only the old can be repeated.

The modern *pathos* of the new dissolves *being* into *process*. The new makes the contemplative life impossible. Contemplation is repetition. The *pathos* of action that goes hand in hand with the emphasis on the new makes the world restless. Arendt understands action as an open process, as a process that lacks a goal that would bring it to rest. Action does not simply envisage a project and then bring it to completion. Rather, the performance of an action 'remains directed toward the constantly renewed actualization of freedom, with new beginnings constantly flowing into what has once been begun'.[39] If action no longer brings about new beginnings, the processes set in motion by freedom begin to rigidify into automatisms that are 'no less ruinous ... than automatic natural processes'.[40] As the power of the new beginning weakens, decline sets in. For this reason, human history for the most part consists of automatic processes that are interrupted only periodically: 'we know that the processes of decline can go on for centuries. Quantitatively, they occupy by far the largest space in recorded history.'[41] Once it is no longer invigorated by new beginnings, an historical epoch is doomed to decline. For Arendt, history has no goal, and only the constant creation of new beginnings can prevent it from ossifying into a rigid, dangerous automatism.

It is not clear that humankind's continued existence on earth really depends on the ongoing reaffirmation of freedom, on the constant creation of new beginnings. The pathos of the new and of new beginnings becomes destructive if it is not contained by *another* spirit, which Nietzsche calls the 'genius of meditation'.[42] It is Nietzsche, with his concept of the revaluation of all values, who truly rejects the blind faith in the new. Although he acknowledges the preachers of the new, he does not lose sight of the need for contemplative life. He thus juxtaposes the great contemplative spirits, the 'farmers of the spirit' as he calls them, with the preachers of the new:

> The strongest and most evil spirits have so far done the most to advance humanity: time and again they rekindled the dozing passions – every ordered society puts the passions to sleep –, time and again they reawakened the sense of comparison, of contradiction, of delight in what is new, daring, unattempted; they forced men to

pit opinion against opinion, ideal model against ideal model. Mostly by force of arms, by toppling boundary stones, by violating pieties – but also by means of new religions and moralities! In every teacher and preacher of what is new we find the same 'mischief' that makes conquerors infamous ... What is new, however, is under all circumstances *evil*, being that which wants to conquer, to overthrow the old boundary stones and pieties; and only what is old is good! In every age the good men are those who bury the old thoughts deeply and make them bear fruit – the farmers of the spirit.[43]

Nietzsche counts the 'great moralists', such as Pascal, Epictetus, Seneca and Plutarch, among the farmers of the spirit.[44] Because of the decline of the *vita contemplativa*, he thinks, our time has few such farmers of the spirit. His explanation of the crisis of modernity rests on the observation that the *genius of contemplation* has left us, that the 'ploughshare of evil', though it has its purpose and, no doubt, is historically useful, has driven the farmers of the spirit away. Arendt is a preacher of the new, and she therefore attributes to the new an absolute value, identifies it with the good as such, as the only thing that can prevent humankind's demise.

Arendt's view transforms *society itself* into the antipode of freedom, because for Arendt society administers mere life. Society is simply the *oikos* – household and family – writ large in public space. She sees society's conformism as deriving from the family, in which there is only ever 'one opinion'.[45] In society, the 'social', mere life, becomes dominant. Society, 'on all its levels, excludes the possibility of action, which formerly was excluded from the household'.[46] Because society is an extension of the private household into the public sphere, where the life of the species is the priority, society comes to be dominated by the survival of the human species, threatening 'the authentic being human of humans', namely the freedom to act, with extinction.[47]

According to Arendt, society culminates in modern mass society: 'Mass society indicates the victory of society as such.'[48] Modern mass society establishes 'rule by nobody'.[49] The 'someone' – the acting subject – is suppressed. In many ways rule by nobody resembles Heidegger's dictatorial 'they' [*man*], which Heidegger also refers to as 'no one'. The rule of Heidegger's 'they' also oppresses the 'possibility of taking action'.[50] In mass society, action is supplanted by a 'certain kind of behaviour' that 'society expects from each of its members . . . imposing innumerable and various rules, all of which tend to "normalize" its members, to make them behave, to exclude spontaneous action or outstanding achievement'.[51]

Equalization is fundamental to society. Arendt juxtaposes 'modern equality, based on the conformism inherent in society', with the equality of the Greek *polis*:

To belong to the few 'equals' (*homoioi*) meant to be permitted to live among one's peers; but the public realm itself, the *polis*, was permeated by a fiercely agonal spirit, where everybody had constantly to distinguish himself from all others, to show through unique deeds or achievements that he was the best of all (*aien aristeúein*). The public realm, in other words, was reserved for individuality; it was the only place where men could show who they really and inexchangeably were.[52]

In mass society, the average 'they', the no one, assumes power. Everything is levelled to produce an ordinary average. Arendt ignores the fact that conformism also characterized the Greek *polis*, which was a 'society', too. The trial of Socrates shows as much.

Arendt's assumption that society results simply from an expansion of the household and family makes it impossible to provide a nuanced analysis of society that identifies different types of society and examines the way they function. 'Rule by nobody' is in fact a result of power structures. Every society, the Greek *polis* included, is a power structure, a regime that turns the human being into a *subject*, that is, someone who is *subjugated*. The body is already an effect of power. This is the insight that underlies Foucault's concept of 'biopower'. Bio*politics* shapes and administers human bodies. In the disciplinary regime that underlies industrial capitalism, biopolitics produces docile bodies. Carefully calculated compulsion runs through every part of the body, turning 'formless clay, an inapt body', into a 'machine'.[53] The docile bodies of the disciplinary regime are not the same as the bodies we optimize with the fitness apps that are available today.

Arendt's social theory is unable to analyse the power structures that produce different types of society – different regimes. It cannot do justice to the transition from the disciplinary to the neoliberal regime, or the development from industrial capitalism to surveillance capitalism. By elevating the political to the status of a unique entity separated from the social, Arendt's theory cuts itself off from the very political and economic power processes that establish a society as a regime.

A new *medium* means *revolution*. It is therefore not only political action that produces novelty, a new order of things. Every new medium leads to a new regime because it establishes new power structures. Industrialization brought about the beginning of the disciplinary regime. Domination itself took on the form of a machine. Disciplinary power inserts the human being into the gear train of the panoptical machine. Digitalization produces the information regime, whose psychopolitics surveils and controls our actions with algorithms and artificial intelligence.

Arendt's notion of mass society cannot capture contemporary social developments. The importance of the mass is in decline. There is a reason why some now talk of a 'society of singularities'. There are constant invocations of creativity and authenticity. Everyone thinks they are unique. Everyone has their own story to tell. Everyone is a performer of their self. The *vita activa* takes the form of a *vita performativa*. There is also a powerful return of emphasis on the new. Novelty, we are told, makes for a full life. The old is not to be trusted. So-called start-ups also invoke creativity and innovation; they promise novelty. From this perspective, Arendt's emphasis on new beginnings sits well with the contemporary mood.

For Arendt, the effect of mass society is to turn everything into the average and, by making it harder to act and speak, to suppress the individual and exceptional. Mass society does not permit 'outstanding achievements' because it 'does not provide a proper space' in which action can aspire to excellence.[54] The 'constituent elements of the public realm, which make it the proper place for human excellence', disappear.[55] Arendt takes mass society to be the ultimate form of society, but mass society is the exact opposite of today's society. We have long since left industrial mass society behind. In the neoliberal regime, society is transformed into the *performance society*, in which individuals seek to competitively improve their performance. The neoliberal regime is not repressive. Now, domination becomes 'smart': it takes the form of a constant compulsion to increase performance. This subtle pressure to perform is interpreted as an expansion of freedom – with disastrous consequences. Believing that we are *realizing ourselves*, we voluntarily exploit ourselves. We worship the cult of the self, in which each is his own priest. This pressure to be authentic is alien to mass society. Mass society was dominated by mass media, but the age of digital media does not suppress the individual's ability to speak. Quite the contrary, everyone is now a producer and broadcaster. Everyone is producing themselves. We become intoxicated with the bewildering amount of communication that is produced.

Arendt believes that what makes humans unique is expressed only in action. The '"who" in contradistinction to "what" somebody is – his qualities, gifts, talents, and shortcomings, which he may display or hide –' is hidden from the actor, for it is only 'implicit' in his words and actions. For this reason, only others can know 'who' someone really is:

> It is more than likely that the 'who', which appears so clearly and unmistakably to others, remains hidden from the person himself, like the *daimon* in Greek religion which accompanies each man throughout his life,

always looking over his shoulder from behind and thus visible only to those he encounters.[56]

Pace Arendt, the Greek *daimon* is not visible to the other. It makes itself known by occasionally speaking personally to its bearer, but third parties know nothing of it. In Plato's *Apology*, Socrates says that the *daimon*'s voice prevents him from acting:

> It may seem strange that while I go around and give this advice privately and interfere in private affairs, I do not venture to go to the assembly and there advise the city. You have heard me give the reason for this in many places. I have a divine or spiritual sign . . . This began when I was a child. It is a voice, and whenever it speaks it turns me away from something I am about to do, but it never encourages me to do anything. This is what has prevented me from taking part in public affairs.[57]

The mysterious voice of the 'spiritual sign', the *daimon*, says: *Stop!* It prevents Socrates from acting. The *daimon* seems to be a *genius of inactivity*.

The Greek *daimon* corresponds to the Roman genius, a protective god who is present at every birth: 'He is called my Genius, because he generated me (*Genius meus nominatur, quia me genuit*).'[58] The genius accompanies us from birth until death. On the one hand he is the closest thing to us; on the other he is what is most impersonal about us, 'the personalization of what, in us, goes beyond and exceeds us'.[59] We owe to it the insight 'that man is not only an ego and an individual consciousness'.[60] The genius 'shatters the ego's pretension to be sufficient unto

78

itself'. Its presence 'prevents us from enclosing ourselves within a substantial identity'.[61]

The properties that make us a *someone* are not *genialis*; that is, they do not accord with the genius. We meet with the genius when we cast off our properties, the mask we wear on the acting stage. The genius reveals the propertyless face that lies behind the mask. This *countenance without properties* is the opposite of the '"who" in contradistinction to "what" somebody is' that Arendt associates with action. Human beings are *propertyless* only once they leave the stage. In the radiance of inactivity, a person is precisely a no one. Inactivity goes along with self-forgetfulness.

Living with the genius means maintaining a relation with the region of not-knowing, non-consciousness. However, the genius does not place experience in the dark, the unconscious, where it is 'sedimented as an uncanny past'.[62] Rather, living with the genius is a *day-bright mysticism* in which the ego is peacefully present at its own dissolution. In being moved by the genius, that is, being *inspired*, we cease to be a *someone* encapsulated in an ego. In the state of being enthused, we detach ourselves from ourselves. *Genialis* is a *standing-beside-oneself*. This is also a *formula for happiness*.

The being-born that commits us to action is *without happiness*. A person who does nothing but act loses the *genius* that inspires and gladdens. Happiness comes from inactivity. This is perhaps why Arendt views human happiness with such contempt: 'For only the *animal laborans*, and neither the craftsman nor the man of action, has ever demanded to be "happy" or thought that mortal men could be happy.'[63]

'Natality', which commits us to action, *entangles us with time*. It is only inactivity that liberates us, even redeems us, from time. It is the genius that embodies a completely different form of life: 'Genius' youthful face and long, fluttering wings signify that he does not know time.'[64] We do not celebrate birthdays to reassure ourselves that we are acting creatures. Rather, birthdays celebrate the epiphany of the genius that lifts us out of time. A birthday celebration is not 'the commemoration of a past day, but, like every true celebration, must be a suspension of time'.[65] Timelessness is the essence of celebration. The time of the festival is a time standing still. We *celebrate* [*begehen*] a festival.[66] We can celebrate only what *stands still* and does not pass [*vergehen*]. We celebrate a festival the way we walk through a magnificent building. Someone who acts has goals before him. He walks in the mode of *moving towards* and *striving for*. Someone who only acts cannot walk around in a festive way, a way that arrests time. Walking around is purposeless. That is what distinguishes it from action, which necessarily has a purpose.

The festive does not form part of Arendt's philosophical vocabulary. Nowhere does she mention it. Her *pathos* of action removes from life every aspect of the festive. Festivals are an expression of abundant life; they are an intense form of life. In the festival, life refers to itself, rather than pursuing aims outside of itself. It suspends action. For this reason, all purposeful activities are prohibited on the Sabbath. Festive silence is life oscillating in itself. It is not the determination to act but the exuberance of the festival that raises us above mere life. The festival takes place outside of the *oikos*. The economic dimension is suspended. The extravagant and extreme forms of behaviour associated with ancient festivals point to this anti-economic character. Action represents a form of survival, but during the festival, life is no longer survival. The festival, more so than action, gives life radiance. Arendt's thought is sealed off from these radiant forms of human existence.

Arendt's *The Human Condition* begins by drawing a distinction between immortality and eternity. Immortality is a lasting, an endurance through time that characterizes both the 'gods' deathless and ageless lives' and nature.[67] Surrounded by infinity, humans, as mortal beings, strive for immortality by creating enduring works. Striving for immortality, Arendt says, is 'the spring and center of the *vita activa*'.[68] Humans achieve immortality on the political stage. The goal of the *vita contemplativa* is not to last or endure in time but to experience an eternity that transcends the contemporary world and time itself. The *vita contemplativa* is situated outside human affairs, that is, outside the political. According to Arendt, however, human beings cannot remain within the experience of eternity. They must return to the contemporary world. But as soon as a thinker leaves behind the experience of eternity and begins to write, he enters the *vita activa*, whose ultimate purpose is immortality. This leads Arendt to the formulation of a very strange thesis:

> For it is obvious that, no matter how concerned a thinker may be with eternity, the moment he sits down to write his thoughts he ceases to be concerned primarily with eternity and shifts his attention to leaving some trace of them. He has entered the *vita activa* and thus has chosen

81

its way of permanence and potential immortality over eternity.[69]

Arendt is therefore astounded by Socrates, who does not write, who voluntarily forgoes immortality. Arendt herself apparently thought and wrote with the intention of gaining immortality. Her very narrow conception of the *vita contemplativa* does not allow for a description of its complex and diverse nature. Even writing can be contemplation, can be something that has nothing to do with the striving for immortality.

Arendt understands the *vita contemplativa* as an escape from the world. She tries to support her thesis with reference to a distorted account of Plato's allegory of the cave:

> The philosopher's experience of the eternal ... can occur only outside the realm of human affairs ... as we know from the Cave parable in Plato's *Republic*, where the philosopher, having liberated himself from the fetters that bound him to his fellow men, leaves the cave in perfect 'singularity', as it were, neither accompanied nor followed by others. ... no living creature can endure it [the experience of the eternal] for any length of time. ... Life itself forces human beings to return to the cave, where they live again, that is, 'are among human beings'.[70]

In fact, Plato's allegory of the cave tells a very different story, that of a philosopher who tears himself free of the chains that tie him to the shadows that he and his fellow captives consider to be the only reality. He leaves the cave to search for the truth. Plato asks Glaucon to imagine what would happen if this philosopher, having seen the truth outside the cave, returned and tried to free the captives from their illusion. The philosopher's actions, which take the form of speaking the truth (*parrhesia*), risk his being killed by the captives. Plato's allegory thus ends as follows: 'And, as for anyone who tried to free them and lead them upward, if they could somehow get their hands on him, wouldn't they kill him?'[71] Plato juxtaposes a regime of truth with the mythical regime embodied by the cave and its shadow images. The philosopher *acts* when, risking his life, he returns to the cave to convince the captives of the truth, but what precedes this action is the philosopher's seeing the truth. Immediately following the allegory of the cave, Plato adds 'that anyone who is to act sensibly in private or public must see it'.[72] Plato's point is therefore that action is preceded by contemplation, which is the path towards knowledge, towards truth. The *vita activa* without the *vita contemplativa* is blind.

Towards the end of *The Human Condition*, Arendt remarks that labour as an absolute value – the victory of the *animal laborans* in the modern age – destroys all other human capacities, most of all the capacity to act. She then, unexpectedly, mentions thinking, which has not featured in the book up to this point. The victory of the *animal laborans* has done the least damage, she says, to thinking. The future of the world does not depend on thinking but on the power of people who act, but thinking is nevertheless not irrelevant to the future of humanity. If we ask which of the various activities of the *vita activa* is the most active – which of them most clearly expresses activity – the answer is that it is thinking. In other words, on the final pages of *The Human Condition*, Arendt declares thinking to be the most active of all human activities.

Arendt seeks to firm up her claim by citing Cato:

> Whoever has any experience in this matter [i.e. thinking; D.S.] will know how right Cato was when he said: *Numquam se plus agere quam nihil cum agent, numquam minus solum esse quam cum solus esset* – 'Never is he more active than when he does nothing, never is he less alone than when he is by himself.'[73]

It is this comment from Cato to which Cicero refers in *De Re Publica* immediately before his paean to the *vita contemplativa*. He calls on his readers to devote themselves to the *vita contemplativa* and to shun the bustle of the masses. For Cicero, thinking is part of the *vita contemplativa*. Arendt thus inadvertently closes her book on the *vita activa* by praising the *vita contemplativa*.

Human existence realizes itself only in a *vita composita*, that is, in the interaction between the *vita activa* and *vita contemplativa*. Saint Gregory teaches:

> Be aware: while a good plan for life requires that one moves from the active to the contemplative life, it is often useful if the soul returns from the contemplative to the active life, in such a way that the flame of contemplation which has been lit in the heart passes on all its perfection to activity. Thus, active life must lead us to contemplation, but contemplation . . . call us back to activity.[74]

Arendt never recognized that it was precisely the loss of the capacity for contemplation that led to the victory of the *animal laborans*, which she criticizes for subjugating all human activities to labour. Against her conviction, the future of humanity depends not on the power of people who act but on the resuscitation of the capacity for contemplation – that is, on the very capacity that does not act. If it does not incorporate the *vita contemplativa*, the *vita activa* degenerates into hyperactivity, and culminates in the burnout not only of the psyche but of the whole planet.

The Coming Society

For Novalis on his 250th birthday

'Every beloved object is the center of a paradise.'[1]

'Does not the rock become a proper thou the very moment I address it?'[2]

Today's crisis of religion cannot be explained simply with reference to the fact that we have lost all faith in God or become suspicious of certain religious doctrines. The crisis suggests that, at a deeper level, we are gradually losing the faculty of contemplation. The intensifying compulsion to produce and communicate makes contemplative lingering difficult. Religion requires a particular form of attention. Malebranche called attention the natural prayer of the soul. Today, souls no longer *pray*. It is the soul's hyperactivity that accounts for the demise of religious experience. The crisis of religion is a crisis of attention.

Vita activa's pathos of action denies any access to religion. Action is not part of religious experience. In *On Religion*, Schleiermacher states that contemplative intuition, which he juxtaposes to action, is the essence of religion: 'It is neither thinking nor acting, but intuition and feeling. It will regard the Universe as it is. It is reverent attention and submission, in child-like passivity, to be stirred and filled by the Universe.'[3] Attending to the world in child-like passivity is a form of inactivity. According to Schleiermacher, religion dissolves 'all activities into an amazed contemplation of the infinite'.[4] Someone who acts has a goal in mind, and loses sight of the totality. Thinking focuses our attention on the thing to be achieved. Only intuition and feeling have access to the universe, that is, to beings in their totality.

Atheism does not rule out religion. For Schleiermacher, it is possible to conceive of religion without God: 'To have religion is to have an intuition of the Universe . . . Now, if you cannot deny that the idea of God suits every intuition, you must also admit that a religion without God might be better than another with God.'[5] What is essential to religion is not God but a desire for the infinite, which finds its fulfilment in the intuition of the universe.

'To listen' is the verb of religion, whereas 'to act' is the verb of history. Careful listening is a form of inactivity in which the ego, the locus of distinctions and delimitations, falls silent. The listening ego immerses *itself* in the totality, in the unlimited, in the infinite. Schleiermacher's talk of the intuition of the universe is expressed in poetic form by some beautiful lines from Hölderlin's *Hyperion*:

87

My whole being stills and listens when the gentle ripple of the breeze plays about my breast. Often, lost in the immensity of blue, I look up into the aether and out into the hallowed sea, . . .

To be one with everything, that is the life of the godhead, that is the heaven of man.

To be one with everything that lives, to return in blissful self-oblivion into the all of nature, that is the summit of thoughts and joys, that is the holy mountain pinnacle, the place of eternal peace.[6]

Those who bring themselves to listen lose *themselves* in the 'all of nature', in the 'immensity of blue', in the 'aether', in the 'hallowed sea'. But those who *produce* themselves, *exhibit* themselves, are incapable of listening carefully, of looking on with child-like passivity. Selflessness is essential to religious experience, so in the age of narcissistic self-production and self-exhibition, religion loses its foundation. Self-production is more damaging to religion than is atheism. Those who hand death to *themselves* participate in the infinite. Schleiermacher writes:

Would they but attempt to surrender their lives out of love for the universe. Would they but strive to annihilate their personality and to live in the One and in the All! Would they but strive to be more than themselves. . . . In the midst of finitude to be one with the infinite and in every moment to be eternal is the immortality of religion.[7]

For Romanticism, nature has a divine radiance. Nature is numinous, and therefore not at our disposal. We violate nature the very moment we look at it as a means for human ends, as a resource. The Romantic understanding of nature may serve as a corrective to our instrumental relationship with nature, which leads inevitably to disaster. Romanticism strives for a reconciliation between humans and nature. In an early version of the preface to *Hyperion*, Hölderlin writes:

> To end this eternal opposition between our self and the world, to bring back the peacefulness of all peace that is above all reasoning, to reunite ourselves with nature into an infinite totality, that is the goal of all our endeavours.[8]

This unification with nature Hölderlin calls 'being'. Without it, 'we would have no intuition of this infinite peace, this, in the singular sense of the word, being; we would not strive to unite nature with us'.[9]

From the perspective of action, rather than being, 'everywhere in the universe man is the centre of all relations, the condition of all existence and the cause of all becoming'.[10] Action never reaches the point of 'being', where 'all opposition ends, where all is one'.[11] Action is characterized by a lack of being. Hölderlin holds the self, the acting subject, responsible for the omnipresent oppositions, the loss of 'being':

> Blissful unity, being, in the singular sense of the word, is lost to us ... We tear ourselves away from the *Hen kai Pan* [universal oneness] of the world in order to create it through ourselves. We have separated from nature, and what once, as one may well believe, was one, is now in opposition with itself.[12]

'Being', that is, *beauty*, results from the *synagogé*, the 'bringing together into One'.[13] As long as reconciliation – infinite peace – is absent, the world lacks beauty. Hölderlin longs for that 'realm' in which 'beauty is the queen'.[14]

In Romanticism, freedom is decoupled from the self. Freedom does not find expression in action but in the passivity of intuition. Acting gives way to careful listening: 'Only when the free impulse of seeing is directed towards the Infinite and goes into the Infinite, is the mind set in unbounded Freedom.'[15] To be free means to unite with the infinity of nature and to live among natural things as among brothers:

'O sun, O you breezes,' I'd then call out, 'with you alone my heart still lives, as amongst brothers!'
Thus I gave myself up more and more to blissful nature, and almost too endlessly. How gladly I'd have become a child to be closer to her! How gladly I'd have known less and become like the pure ray of light to be closer to her!'[16]

The religious moment is the moment when freedom turns into nature: 'Religion begins to breathe where freedom itself has already become nature again.'[17] Nature opens the eyes of the subject that thinks itself free and sovereign, giving it the ability to *look*. The genuinely Romantic moment occurs when, in the face of nature, the subject abandons its sovereignty and begins to weep. Nature allows the subject to realize its own naturalness:

Rather than that, as Kant thought, spirit in the face of nature becomes aware of its own superiority, it becomes aware of its own natural essence. This is the moment when the subject, vis-à-vis the sublime, is moved to tears. Recollection of nature breaks the arrogance of his self-positing: 'My tears well up; earth, I am returning to you.' With that, the self exits, spiritually, from its imprisonment in itself.[18]

Tears 'break the spell that the subject casts over nature'.[19] In tears, the subject admits that it belongs to the earth.

The Romantic notion of natural beauty does not denote something that the subject simply likes. Such immediate pleasure is merely the pleasure that the subject takes in itself. Natural beauty unsettles the subject that posits itself as absolute and disrupts its self-satisfaction, and for this reason natural beauty can be experienced only by way of pain. The pain is the *rift in the subject* through which the *other of the subject* announces itself: 'The pain in the face of beauty, nowhere more visceral than in the experience of nature, is as much the longing for what beauty promises.'[20] To the extent that it hints at the condition of being, in which human beings are reconciled with nature, natural beauty has a utopian potential.

The early Romantics' idea of freedom is a corrective, even an antidote, for today's notion of individual freedom. Romantic freedom is not based on wanting-*oneself*, or a will-to-*self*, but a *being-with* or *shared willing*:

Shared willing is rather a letting oneself go and releasing oneself into being. Shared willing is a having to, but

91

a having to ... that stems from an *open belonging to beyng* and returns back *into it*. This belonging, however, is the innermost essence of freedom.[21]

Freedom as belonging does justice to the original idea of freedom. Etymologically, the word 'free' means *to be among friends*. Both 'freedom' and 'friend' have the Indo-Germanic root *'fri'*, meaning *'to love'*. *Freedom is friendliness*. This is why Hölderlin takes friendliness, which suspends all separation and isolation, to be a divine principle: 'Yes. As long as kindliness, which is pure, remains in his heart not unhappily a man may compare himself with the divinity.'[22]

For Novalis, nature is not an inanimate *it* but a living *you*. A connection with nature can be established only by *invocation*. Saving nature means leading her out of her existence as an *it*, which exposes her to ruthless exploitation, and addressing her as a *you*. Every thing becomes a *you* when we *invoke* it. The early Romantics believed that nature is a feeling, thinking and speaking being. For Schelling, it is visible spirit, and the human spirit is invisible nature. Her language, however, consists of hieroglyphs that remain unintelligible to humans as long as they are alienated from nature. She reveals her secrets to those who approach her with love and imagination.

The Romantic conception of nature, which takes even inanimate things to have souls, provides an effective corrective to our instrumental understanding of nature. The Romantic perception prevents us from viewing nature as a resource that only serves human purposes. According to Novalis, there is a deep sympathy between humans and nature. Looking more deeply, we can see manifold correspondences between humans and nature. Even thinking is not categorically different from nature. Novalis assumes that there is an analogy between the play of intellectual reflection and the play of nature. The human body reflects nature in microcosm. There is a mysterious analogy between humans and nature.

To the early Romantics, nature appeared playful. It is free from purpose and use. Its character is inactivity. Nature is 'like a child lost in play with not a thought in the world' and 'effortless too, so blissfully at peace'.[23] Similarly, true language is not a means to an end, not a means of communication. It refers to itself and plays with itself. It speaks for the sake of speaking. In poetry, it sheds all purpose. It does not *work*. For Novalis, the glory of language unfolds only beyond meaning and understanding:

> Speech is not understood, because speech does not understand itself, and will not be understood. Genuine Sanscrit speaks for the sake of speaking, because speech is its pleasure and its essence.
>
> . . . Holy Writ needs no commentary. Whoso speaks truly is full of everlasting life, and his Evangel seems to us wonderfully linked with Genuine Secrets, for it is a harmony out of the Universal Symphony.[24]

The Romantics do not simply project their subjective feelings, desires and longings on to a nature that is in itself without life or soul. This is not a case of anthropomorphism, of subjectivizing nature. Rather, nature has its own inwardness, a 'Gemüt', that is, a heart and soul.

> Only the poets have felt what Nature can be to man
> . . . For them Nature has all the variability of a limitless
> soul, she surprises them more than the most ready and
> clever man by her ingenious turns and incidents, by her
> meetings (confluences) and her deviations, by her great
> ideas and vagaries.[25]

Nature is 'that one poem of the godhead . . . of which we, too, are part and flower'.[26] Novalis sees nature as an artist with an 'artistic instinct'. Novalis is convinced that distinguishing between nature and art is erroneous 'idle talk'.[27]

German Romanticism is more than 'lonely forests and the magic of woods, rushing millstreams', 'the night watchman's call and murmuring wells, the ruin of a palace with a garden that has fallen back to nature, in which marble statues weather and crumble', nor is it a return to the 'ancient customs of home', still less to a 'strong national feeling' or a 'strong new Germanness'.[28] Early Romanticism represented a universalist aesthetic-political idea. Novalis advocates a radical universalism: the establishment of a 'world family' beyond nation and identity.[29] He was animated by a longing for reconciliation and harmony, by the idea of eternal peace.

As Novalis saw it, nothing in the world stands in isolation. Everything flows into everything else. Everything is entangled. For Novalis, poetry is a medium of unification, reconciliation and love. Poetry releases an *intensity* that pulls things out of their isolation and unites them in a beautiful society:

Poetry elevates each single thing through a particular combination with the rest of the whole . . . poetry shapes the beautiful society – the world family – the beautiful household of the universe.

. . . The individual lives in the whole and the whole in the individual. Through poetry there arises the highest sympathy and common activity, the most intimate *communion* of the finite and the infinite.[30]

The goal is a *community of the living*. The whole is the 'instrument of the individual and the individual the instrument of the whole'.[31] Individual and whole permeate each other. Novalis is convinced that separation and isolation ultimately make people ill. Poetry is an art of healing, the 'great art of the construction of transcendental health'.[32] Novalis thus calls the poet a 'transcendental physician'.[33]

Romanticizing the world means giving it back its magic, its mystery, even its dignity. It creates intensity:

The world must be made Romantic. In that way one can find the original meaning again. . . . By endowing the commonplace with a higher meaning, the ordinary with a mysterious appearance, the known with the dignity of the unknown, the finite with the semblance of the infinite, I am making it Romantic.[34]

A Romanticized world would reveal the 'Gemüt', the heart and soul, the *inside of the outside* world from which we are estranged. Novalis calls out: 'Thou didst to life my noble impulse warm, / Deep in the spirit of the world to look.'[35] Romanticization is enchantment. It is an antidote to the profanation of the world, and as such it turns the world into a 'Roman', a novel. Novalis would have said: into a *fairy tale*. With the informatization and digitalization of the world, profanation reaches its apex. Everything takes on the form of data, becomes countable. Information is not narrative but additive. It cannot be condensed into a novel – a recounting. Digital technology is based on binary counting. The French for 'digital' is *numérique*: numerical. Counting is precisely the opposite of recounting. *Numbers do not tell anything.* They are the *degree zero of meaning.*

It is a mistake to reject as rapturous, untimely, or regressive the Romantic longing for a connection with the whole, with nature, with the universe. For Walter Benjamin, this longing is fundamental to humanity:

> The ancients' intercourse with the cosmos had been different: the ecstatic trance [*Rausch*]. . . . This means, however, that man can be in ecstatic contact with the cosmos only communally. It is the dangerous error of modern men to regard this experience as unimportant and avoidable, and to consign it to the individual as the poetic rapture of starry nights. It is not; its hour strikes again and again.[36]

Novalis's position is a Romantic messianism. Everywhere he looks he sees 'the holy time of eternal peace', a 'great time of reconciliation', 'a prophetic, consoling time, working miracles and healing wounds, and sparking the flame of eternal life'.[37] These are 'only hints, disjointed and rough', yet together they signal the 'ardent conception of a new Messiah'.[38] They announce a new age, a new way of seeing, an altogether different form of life.

In *The Coming Community*, Agamben mentions a parable about the coming of the Messiah that Walter Benjamin had apparently told one evening to Ernst Bloch. Bloch tells the story as follows:

> A rabbi, a real cabalist, once said that in order to establish the reign of peace it is not necessary to destroy everything nor to begin a completely new world. It is sufficient to displace this cup or this bush or this stone just a little, and thus everything. But this small displacement is so difficult to achieve and its measure is so difficult to find that, with regard to the world, humans are incapable of it and it is necessary that the Messiah come.[39]

Benjamin's version of the story goes like this:

> The Hasidim have a saying about the world to come. Everything there will be arranged just as it is with us. The room we have now will be just the same in the world to come; where our child lies sleeping, it will sleep in the world to come. The clothes we are wearing we shall also wear in the next world. Everything will be the same as here – only a little bit different.[40]

In the world to come, everything will be as it is now, and nothing will be added, but it will be a little bit different. It is unclear what this 'little bit different' means. Could it mean that things in the world to come will behave altogether differently towards one other, that they will enter into new relationships?

There is a fragment by Novalis that reads like the rabbi's parable: 'In the future world everything is as it is in the former world – and yet everything is quite different.'[41] As far as the facts are concerned, the future world is identical with the present reality. Nothing is added, and nothing is removed. And yet everything is *quite different*. Unlike the Cabbalist rabbi, however, Novalis hints at what the future world might look like. In the same fragment, he speaks of it as '*reasonable* chaos'. The future world is topsy-turvy, but in a reasonable way. Things touch and permeate each other. Nothing is isolated. Nothing rests in itself. Nothing affirms itself. There are no rigid boundaries that separate things from each other. They open themselves up to each other. We could also say: they become *friendly* towards one another. Their *friendly smile* releases the hold of identity. They flow into and mix with one another. The world shines in this *friendly topsy-turviness*, in this '*reasonable* chaos'.

Novalis's *coming society* is based on an *ethos of friendliness* that removes separation, division and estrangement. It is a time of reconciliation and peace. In *The Disciples at Saïs*, he writes:

Soon he became aware of the inter-relation of all things, of conjunctions, of coincidences. Ere long he saw nothing singly. The perceptions of his senses thronged together in great variegated Pictures; he heard, saw, felt and thought simultaneously. He took pleasure in bringing strangers together. Sometimes the stars became men to him, men as stars; stones were as animals, clouds as plants.[42]

In the coming realm of peace, humans and nature are reconciled with each other. Human beings are but *fellow citizens* in a *republic of the living* – of plants, animals, stones, clouds and stars.

NOTES

Views of Inactivity

1 Friedrich Nietzsche, *Human, All Too Human: A Book for Free Spirits*, Cambridge: Cambridge University Press, 1996, p. 132.
2 Karl Kerényi, *Antike Religion*, Munich and Vienna: Klett-Cotta, 1971, p. 62.
3 Theodor W. Adorno, *Aesthetic Theory*, London and New York: Continuum, 2002, p. 294.
4 Guy Debord, *The Society of the Spectacle*, Berkeley: Bureau of Public Secrets, 2014, p. 84.
5 'Community' in English in the original.
6 Debord, *The Society of the Spectacle*, p. 84.
7 Theodor W. Adorno, *Minima Moralia*, London: Verso, 2005, p. 119.
8 Walter Benjamin, *The Arcades Project*, Cambridge MA: Harvard University Press, 1999, p. 425.
9 Ibid., p. 880.

10 Giorgio Agamben, *Nudities*, Stanford: Stanford University Press, 2011, p. 111.

11 Gaston Bachelard, *The Psychoanalysis of Fire*, London: Routledge, 1964, pp. 14f.

12 See Kerényi, *Antike Religion*, p. 48.

13 Agamben, *Nudities*, p. 107.

14 Ibid.

15 Walter Benjamin, 'Falernian Wine and Stockfish', in *Selected Writings, Vol. 2: Part 1, 1927–1930*, Cambridge MA: Harvard University Press, 1999, p. 360.

16 Ibid.

17 'Power nap' in English in the original.

18 Marcel Proust, *In Search of Lost Time, Vol. IV: Sodom and Gomorrha*, New York: The Modern Library, 1999, p. 216.

19 Marcel Proust, *In Search of Lost Time, Vol VI: Time Regained*, London: Vintage, 1996, p. 246.

20 Marcel Proust, *In Search of Lost Time, Vol. V: The Captive*, New York: The Modern Library, 1993, p. 456.

21 Proust, *In Search of Lost Time, Vol. VI: Time Regained*, p. 216.

22 Benjamin, *The Arcades Project*, p. 105.

23 Walter Benjamin, 'The Storyteller', in *Illuminations*, New York: Schocken Books, 1968, pp. 83–109; here: p. 91.

24 Ibid.

25 Martin Heidegger, 'The Nature of Language', in *On the Way to Language*, New York: Harper & Row, 1971, pp. 57–108; here: p. 57.

26 Benjamin, 'The Storyteller', p. 91.

27 Transl. note: 'long whiling' translates 'lange Weile', alluding to the German for boredom, 'Langeweile'.

28 Walter Benjamin, *Gesammelte Schriften, Vol. II*, Frankfurt am Main: Suhrkamp, 1991, p. 1287. – Transl. note: following Benjamin, Han plays on the German terms 'Blätter',

a term for journals and papers, and 'Blätterwald', literally a wood or forest of journals and newspapers, a metaphor used to refer to an excessive amount of printed media.

29 'L'attente commence quand il n'y a plus rien à attendre, ni même la fin de l'attente. L'attente ignore et détruit ce qu'elle attend. L'attente attend rien.' Maurice Blanchot, *L'attente, l'oubli*, Paris: Gallimard, 2000, p. 39; my translation, D.S.

30 Maurice Blanchot, *The Space of Literature*, Lincoln: University of Nebraska Press, 1989, p. 12.

31 Ibid., p. 91.

32 Friedrich Nietzsche, *The Will to Power: Selections from the Notebooks of the 1880s*, London: Penguin, 2017, p. 351.

33 Heinrich von Kleist, 'On the Marionette Theatre', *The Drama Review*, Vol. 16, No. 3, The 'Puppet' Issue (Sept. 1972), pp. 22–6; here: p. 22 and p. 24.

34 Ibid., p. 22 (transl. amended)

35 Ibid., p. 26.

36 Benjamin, 'Practice', from *Ibizan Sequence*, in *Selected Writings, Vol. 2: Part 2*, pp. 590–91; here: p. 591.

37 Ibid. (transl. modified).

38 Roland Barthes, 'Dare to Be Lazy', in *The Grain of the Voice: Interviews 1962–1980*, New York: Hill and Wang, 1985, pp. 338–45; here: pp. 341f.

39 Walter Benjamin, *Berlin Childhood around 1900*, Cambridge MA: Harvard University Press, 2006, pp. 134f.

40 Walter Benjamin, *Gesammelte Schriften, Vol. VI*, Frankfurt am Main: Suhrkamp, 1991, p. 194.

41 Benjamin, *The Arcades Project*, p. 105.

42 Ibid., p. 106.

43 Walter Benjamin, 'The Handkerchief', in *The Storyteller Essays*, New York: The New York Review of Books, 2020, pp. 28–32; here: p. 28.

44 Friedrich Nietzsche, *Nachgelassene Fragmente 1880–1882*,

Sämtliche Werke, Kritische Studienausgabe, Vol. 9, Berlin and New York: De Gruyter, 1988, p. 24.

45 Gilles Deleuze, 'Mediators', in *Negotiations 1972–1990*, New York: Columbia University Press, 1995, pp. 122–34; here: p. 129.

46 Nietzsche, *Human, All Too Human*, p. 132.

47 Ibid.

48 Ibid., p. 133.

49 Giorgio Agamben, *The Kingdom and the Glory: For a Genealogy of Economy and Government*, Stanford: Stanford University Press, 2011, pp. 251f.

50 Michel Butor, interview in *Die Zeit*, 12 July 2012.

51 Karl Marx, *Grundrisse: Introduction to the Critique of Political Economy*, London: Vintage, 1973, p. 650.

52 Ibid.

53 Gilles Deleuze, *Pure Immanence: Essays on A Life*, New York: Zone Books, 2001, p. 27.

54 Ibid., p. 30.

55 Gilles Deleuze and Félix Guattari, *What is Philosophy?*, New York: Columbia University Press, 1994, p. 213.

56 Peter Handke, 'Essay on Tiredness', in *The Jukebox and Other Essays on Storytelling*, New York: Farrar, Straus and Giroux, 1994, pp. 3–46; here: p. 42.

57 Ibid., p. 37 and p. 15.

58 Ibid., p. 41 (transl. amended).

59 Robert Musil, *The Man Without Qualities, Vol. II: From the Posthumous Papers*, New York: Vintage, 1996, p. 1409.

60 Ibid., pp. 1328f.

61 Ibid., p. 1184 and p. 1336.

62 Ibid., p. 828.

63 Ibid., p. 827.

64 Handke, 'Essay on Tiredness', p. 38.

65 Peter Handke, *Die Geschichte des Bleistifts*, Frankfurt am Main: Suhrkamp, 1985, p. 235.

66 Paul Cézanne, *Conversations with Cézanne*, Berkeley: University of California Press, 2001, p. 122.

67 Joachim Gasquet, *Cézanne*, Paris: Les Éditions Bernheim-Jeune, 1921, p. 102.

68 Cézanne, *Conversations with Cézanne*, p. 156.

69 Ibid., p. 115.

70 Ibid., p. 157.

71 Maurice Merleau-Ponty, *Sense and Non-Sense*, Evanston IL: Northwestern University Press, 1964. p. 16 (emphasis added, B.-C. Han).

72 Cézanne, *Conversations with Cézanne*, p. 119.

73 Ibid.

74 Ibid., p. 111.

75 Lorenz Dittmann, 'Zur Kunst Cézannes', in *Festschrift Kurt Badt zum siebzigsten Geburtstage*, ed. Martin Gosebruch, Berlin: De Gruyter, 1961, pp. 190–212; here: p. 196.

A Marginal Note on Zhuangzi

1 Zhuangzi, *The Complete Works of Zhuangzi*, New York: Columbia University Press, 2013, p. 20.

2 Masanobu Fukuoka, *The One-Straw Revolution*, Emmaus PA: Rodale Press, 1978, p. 19.

3 Ibid., p. 34.

4 Martin Heidegger, 'Overcoming Metaphysics', in *The End of Philosophy*, New York: Harper & Row, 1973, pp. 84–110; here: p. 110.

5 Ibid., p. 109.

From Acting to Being

1 Walter Benjamin, 'Theses on the Philosophy of History', in *Illuminations: Essays and Reflections*, New York: Schocken Books, 2007, pp. 253–64; here: pp. 257f.

2 Hannah Arendt, 'Natur und Geschichte', in *Zwischen*

Vergangenheit und Zukunft: Übungen im politischen Denken I, Munich: Piper, 2012, pp. 54–79; here: p. 78. – Transl. note: I have translated from the German edition, as the English and German versions differ substantially. See the list of corresponding passages in the German edition pp. 434ff. The corresponding passage in the English edition runs: 'If, therefore, by starting natural processes, we have begun to act into nature, we have manifestly begun to carry our own unpredictability into that realm which we used to think of as ruled by inexorable laws. The "iron law" of history was always only a metaphor borrowed from nature; and the fact is that this metaphor no longer convinces us because it has turned out that natural science can by no means be sure of an unchallengeable rule of law in nature as soon as men, scientists and technicians, or simply builders of the human artifice, decide to interfere and no longer leave nature to herself.' Hannah Arendt, 'The Concept of History: Ancient and Modern', in *Between Past and Future: Exercises in Political Thought*, New York: Viking Press, 1961, pp. 41–90; here: p. 61.

3 Arendt, 'Natur und Geschichte', p. 79. Transl. note: See Arendt, 'The Concept of History: Ancient and Modern', p. 63: 'It is beyond doubt that the capacity to act is the most dangerous of all human abilities and possibilities, and it is also beyond doubt that the self-created risks mankind faces today have never been faced before. Considerations like these are not at all meant to offer solutions or to give advice. At best, they might encourage sustained and closer reflection on the nature and the intrinsic potentialities of action, which never before has revealed its greatness and its dangers so openly.'

4 Benjamin, *The Arcades Project*, p. 473.

5 Ibid., p. 544.

6 Martin Heidegger, 'Science and Reflection', in *The*

Question Concerning Technology and Other Essays, New York: Garland Publishing, 1977, pp. 155–82; here: p. 180. – Transl. note: Heidegger plays on the fact that 'Sinn' can mean both 'sense' and 'direction', as in 'Uhrzeigersinn', clockwise direction, or 'Ortssinn', a person's sense of orientation (i.e. knowing in which direction to go).

7 Martin Heidegger, *Ponderings II–VII, Black Notebooks 1931–1938*, Bloomington: Indiana University Press, 2016, p. 324 (transl. modified).

8 Martin Heidegger, *Contributions to Philosophy (Of the Event)*, Bloomington: Indiana University Press, 2012, p. 19.

9 Martin Heidegger, *What is Called Thinking?*, New York: Harper & Row, 1968, p. 207.

10 Heidegger, *On the Way to Language*, p. 101.

11 Ibid., p. 93.

12 Martin Heidegger, *Country Path Conversations*, Bloomington: Indiana University Press, 2010, p. 147.

13 Ibid.

14 Heidegger, 'Science and Reflection', p. 181.

15 Martin Heidegger, *Being and Time*, Oxford: Basil Blackwell, 1962, p. 176.

16 Martin Heidegger, *What is Philosophy?*, Lanham: Rowman & Littlefield, 2003, p. 77.

17 Ibid., p. 73.

18 Ibid., pp. 75–7.

19 Heidegger, *Contributions to Philosophy (Of the Event)*, p. 19 (transl. amended).

20 Ibid. (transl. amended).

21 Ibid., p. 83.

22 Heidegger, *Country Path Conversations*, p. 97.

23 Martin Heidegger, 'The Pathway', in Thomas Sheehan (ed.), *Heidegger: The Man and the Thinker*, Chicago: Precedent Publishing, 1981, pp. 69–71; here: p. 71.

24 Martin Heidegger, 'Letter on "Humanism"', in *Pathmarks*,

Cambridge: Cambridge University Press, 1998, pp. 239–76; here: 241.

25 Martin Heidegger, 'Building Dwelling Thinking', in *Poetry, Language, Thought*, New York: Harper & Row, 1971, pp. 141–59; here: p. 148.

26 Ibid., p. 147 (transl. amended; German added).

27 Martin Heidegger, *Hölderlin's Hymn 'Remembrance'*, Bloomington: Indiana University Press, 2018, p. 66.

28 Heidegger, *Ponderings II–VII, Black Notebooks 1931–1938*, p. 170.

29 See Heidegger, *Being and Time*, pp. 228ff.

30 Ibid., p. 232.

31 Ibid., p. 315 and p. 164.

32 Martin Heidegger, *The Fundamental Concepts of Metaphysics: World, Finitude, Solitude*, Bloomington: Indiana University Press, 1995, p. 140.

33 Ibid., p. 141.

34 Ibid., p. 149.

35 Heidegger, *Being and Time*, p. 308.

36 See Byung-Chul Han, *Tod und Alterität*, Munich: Wilhelm Fink, 2002.

37 Heidegger, *Being and Time*, p. 101.

38 Heidegger, *Hölderlin's Hymn 'Remembrance'*, p. 58.

39 Heidegger, 'What is Metaphysics?', in *Pathmarks*, pp. 82–96; here: p. 87.

40 Heidegger, *Hölderlin's Hymn 'Remembrance'*, pp. 59f.

41 Martin Heidegger, 'Andenken an Marcelle Mathieu', in *Reden und andere Zeugnisse eines Lebensweges, Gesamtausgabe, Vol. 16*, Frankfurt am Main: Vittorio Klostermann, 2000, pp. 731–3; here: p. 731.

42 Heidegger, *Hölderlin's Hymn 'Remembrance'*, p. 109.

43 Heidegger, 'Andenken an Marcelle Mathieu', p. 733.

44 Heidegger, *Country Path Conversations*, p. 117.

45 Heidegger, 'Andenken an Marcelle Mathieu', p. 732.

1 Rainer Maria Rilke, *Duino Elegies* (first elegy), in *Duino Elegies and the Sonnets to Orpheus*, Boston: Houghton Mifflin, 1975, p. 9. – Transl. note: my translation. The German is 'Denn Bleiben ist nirgends' (p. 8), rendered in the English translation as 'Because to stay is to be nowhere', a just about possible interpretation that, however, does not fit with Han's reading.

2 Arendt, 'The Concept of History: Ancient and Modern', p. 44.

3 Rainer Maria Rilke, *Selected Poems*, Oxford: Oxford University Press, 2011, p. 129 (transl. amended). 'Berge ruhn, von Sternen überprächtigt; / aber auch in ihnen flimmert Zeit. / Ach, in meinem wilden Herzen nächtigt / obdachlos die Unverganglichkeit.' Ibid., p. 128.

4 Ibid., p. 129. 'Wunderliches Wort: die Zeit vertreiben! / Sie zu *halten*, wäre das Problem. / Denn, wen ängstigts nicht: / wo ist ein Bleiben, wo ein endlich *Sein* in alledem?' Ibid., p. 128.

5 Niklas Luhmann, *Entscheidungen in der 'Informationsgesellschaft'*, at: https://www.fen.ch/texte/gast_luhmann_informationsgesellschaft.htm.

6 Friedrich Nietzsche, *Unpublished Writings from the Period of* Unfashionable Observations, Stanford: Stanford University Press, 1995, p. 272.

7 Hans-Georg Gadamer, 'The Relevance of the Beautiful: Art as Play, Symbol, and Festival', in *The Relevance of the Beautiful and Other Essays*, Cambridge: Cambridge University Press, 1986, p. 32.

8 Menander, *Plays and Fragments*, London: Penguin, 1987, Fragment 416a from *The Changeling [Hypoboimaios]*.

9 Diogenes Laërtius, *The Lives and Opinions of Eminent Philosophers*, London: G. Bell and Sons, 1915, p. 60.

10 Homer, *Iliad*, London: Cassell and Company, 1909, p. 335.

11 Thomas Aquinas, *Summa Theologiae*, II.II, Q. 181, art. 1: 'active life is a disposition to the contemplative life' (at: http://www.logicmuseum.com/wiki/Authors/Thomas _Aquinas/Summa_Theologiae/Part_IIb/Q181).

12 Thomas Aquinas, *Summa Theologiae*, II.II, Q. 180, art. 4 (at: http://www.logicmuseum.com/wiki/Authors/Thomas_Aquinas/Summa_Theologiae/Part_IIb/Q180).

13 Thomas Aquinas, *Quodlibetal Questions*, VIII, Q. 9, art. 1: 'Vision is the whole reward' (at: https://aquinas.cc/la/en/~QVIII.Q9.A1.T).

14 Thomas Aquinas, *Commentary on Aristotle's Nicomachean Ethics*, Book 10, Lecture 11, section 2101 (at: https://aquinas.cc/la/en/~Eth.Bk10.L11.n2099).

15 Augustine, *The City of God against the Pagans*, Cambridge: Cambridge University Press, 1998, p. 1182 (transl. amended).

16 'For where the love is, there the eye is.' Thomas Aquinas, *Commentary on Sentences*, Book 3, Distinction 35, Question 1, Article 1, Response to Quaestiuncula 1 (at: https://aquinas.cc/la/en/~Sent.III.D35.Q1.A2.qa1.C.)

17 Rainer Maria Rilke, 'O tell us, poet', in *Selected Poems*, New York: Routledge, 1990, p. 209.

18 Transl. note: the expression 'endlich Sein' can mean both 'being finite' and to 'finally be'.

19 Rilke, *Sonnets to Orpheus* (Part 1, no. 7), in *Duino Elegies and the Sonnets to Orpheus*, p. 97.

20 Ibid., *Duino Elegies* (seventh elegy), p. 47.

21 Ibid.

22 Kerényi, *Antike Religion*, p. 47.

23 Ibid., p. 62 (emphasis added, B.-C. Han).

24 Transl. note: the German 'Hochzeit' (wedding) literally means 'high time'.

25 Gadamer, 'The Relevance of the Beautiful', p. 39.

26 Kerényi, *Antike Religion*, p. 111.

27 Harpocration, § Th19 (Thargelia); at: https://topostext .org/work.php?work_id=537.

28 Kerényi, *Antike Religion*, p. 111.

29 Aristotle, *Nicomachean Ethics*, Oxford: Oxford University Press, 2009, p. 195 (1177b).

30 Ibid., p. 197 (1178b).

31 Ibid.

32 Ibid., p. 194 (1177a).

33 George Santayana, *The Middle Span, Vol. II: Persons and Places*, New York: Charles Scribner's Sons, 1942, p. 142.

The Pathos *of Action*

1 Vilém Flusser, *Kommunikologie weiter denken*, Frankfurt am Main: Fischer, 2009, p. 236.

2 Abraham Joshua Heschel, *The Sabbath: Its Meaning for Modern Man*, New York: Farrar, Straus and Giroux, 1951, p. 12.

3 *Rashi's Commentary on Genesis*, here: Genesis 2:3; at: https://www.chabad.org/library/bible_cdo/aid/8166/sh owrashi/true

4 Heschel, *The Sabbath*, pp. 54f.

5 Hannah Arendt, 'The Meaning of Revolution', in *On Revolution*, London: Penguin, 1990, pp. 21–59; here: p. 34.

6 Hannah Arendt, *The Human Condition*, Chicago: University of Chicago Press, 1998 [1958], p. 177.

7 Ibid., p. 197.

8 Ibid., pp. 197f.

9 This passage is not part of the English edition; the corresponding passage is the second paragraph on p. 198 of *The Human Condition*.

10 Ibid., pp. 197f. The English edition differs signifi-

cantly. The terms 'Lebensgefühl' [feeling for life] and 'Wirklichkeitsgefühl' [feeling for reality] have no equivalents in it.

11 Flusser, *Kommunikologie weiter denken*, p. 237.

12 Tonio Hölscher, 'Die griechische Polis und ihre Räume: Religiöse Grenzen und Übergänge', in Martin A. Guggisberg (ed.), *Grenzen in Ritual und Kult der Antike*, Basle: Schwabe Verlag, 2013, pp. 47–68; here: p. 54.

13 Martin Heidegger, 'Zu den Inseln der Ägäis: 1967', in *Gesamtausgabe*, *Vol. 75*, Frankfurt am Main: Vittorio Klostermann, 2000, pp. 247–73; p. 251.

14 Arendt, *The Human Condition*, p. 43.

15 Judith N. Shklar, 'Hannah Arendt as Pariah', in *Political Thought and Political Thinkers*, Chicago: University of Chicago Press, 1998, pp. 363–75; here: p. 371.

16 Plato, *Apology*, in *Complete Works*, Indianapolis: Hackett, 1997, pp. 17–36; here: p. 29 (31d-e).

17 Arendt, *On Revolution*, p. 281. – Transl. note: the English and German editions differ. Where the German has: 'woran diese Menschen sich hielten, um von der Trauer des Lebendigen nicht übermannt zu werden und aus der Finsternis der Kreatur in die Helle des Menschlichen zu gelangen' [what enabled these people not to succumb to the sadness of life, and to move from the darkness of the creaturely into the brightness of the human], the English has: 'what it was that enabled ordinary men, young and old, to bear life's burden'. Hannah Arendt, *Über die Revolution*, Munich: Piper, 2011 [1963], p. 362.

18 Arendt, *On Revolution*, p. 281. – Transl. note: 'fenced-in' added; see next paragraph.

19 Arendt, *The Human Condition*, p. 19. – Transl. note: I follow the German edition; see *Vita Activa oder Vom tätigen Leben*, Munich: Piper, 1981 [1967], p. 24. In both editions, the passage speaks of the distinction between

man and animal running right through the human species itself. But the English edition puts the part corresponding to the quotation – following Heraclitus – as only those '"who prefer immortal fame to mortal things" are really human'.

20 Arendt, *The Human Condition*, p. 37.

21 Ibid., p. 176. – Transl. note: 'a world that already existed before we were born' omitted in the German edition; see *Vita Activa*, p. 165.

22 Arendt, *On Revolution*, p. 34.

23 Hannah Arendt, '"The Freedom to Be Free": The Conditions and Meaning of Revolution', in *Thinking without a Banister: Essays in Understanding 1953–1975*, New York: Schocken, 2018, pp. 368–86; here: pp. 377.

24 Ibid., pp. 380f.

25 Ibid., p. 377.

26 Ibid. – Transl. note: the full sentence of the English edition puts a different slant on this: 'The difference, then, was that the American Revolution – because of the institution of slavery and the belief that slaves belonged to a different "race" – overlooked the existence of the miserable, and with it the formidable task of liberating those who were not so much constrained by political oppression as the sheer necessities of life.'

27 'Hannah Arendt on Hannah Arendt', in *Thinking without a Banister*, pp. 443–75; here: p. 457.

28 Hannah Arendt: 'Totalitarian Imperialism: Reflections on the Hungarian Revolution', in *The Journal of Politics*, Vol. 20, No. 1 (1958), pp. 5–43; here: p. 29 (transl. modified). – Transl. note: the passage 'and for that very reason should play no role in the polis, the realm of the political' is an addition to the German text; see *Die Ungarische Revolution und der totalitäre Imperialismus*, Munich: Piper, 1958, pp. 41f.

29 Arendt, *On Revolution*, p. 65.

30 Arendt, 'Revolution and Freedom: A Lecture', in *Thinking without a Banister*, pp. 332–54; here: p. 352.

31 Arendt, *On Revolution*, p. 114.

32 Arendt, 'Revolution and Freedom: A Lecture', p. 352.

33 Ibid.

34 Jean Ziegler, *Betting on Famine*, New York: The New Press, 2013, p. xiii.

35 Arendt, 'The Freedom to Be Free', p. 383.

36 Arendt, *The Human Condition*, p. 247.

37 Arendt, *On Revolution*, p. 46.

38 Søren Kierkegaard, *Repetition*, in *Fear and Trembling/ Repetition*, Princeton: Princeton University Press, 1983, pp. 125–231; here: p. 132.

39 Arendt, 'Freedom and Politics: A Lecture', in *Thinking without a Banister*, pp. 220–44; here: p. 242.

40 Ibid., p. 243.

41 Ibid.

42 Nietzsche, *Human, All Too Human*, p. 132.

43 Friedrich Nietzsche, *The Gay Science*, Cambridge: Cambridge University Press, 2001, p. 32.

44 Nietzsche, *Human, All Too Human*, p. 131.

45 Arendt, *The Human Condition*, p. 39.

46 Ibid., p. 40. – Transl. note: the German edition has 'in allen ihren Entwicklungsstadien' [throughout all of its developmental stages] instead of 'on all its levels'.

47 Arendt, *Vita Activa*, p. 46. – Transl. note: The English edition does not contain this qualification and speaks only of 'humanity' as threatened with extinction: *The Human Condition*, p. 46.

48 Arendt, *Vita Activa*, p. 42. – Transl. note: the full German sentence runs: 'Die Massengesellschaft zeigt den Sieg der Gesellschaft überhaupt an; sie ist das Stadium, in dem es außerhalb der Gesellschaft stehende Gruppen

schlechterdings nicht mehr gibt.' The second, unquoted, part of the sentence brings it closer to the corresponding English passage, which, however, lacks something of the German's pithiness: 'with the emergence of mass society, the realm of the social has finally, after several centuries of development, reached the point where it embraces and controls all members of a given community equally and with equal strength.' *The Human Condition*, p. 41.

49 Arendt, *The Human Condition*, p. 40.

50 Heidegger, *Being and Time*, p. 340.

51 Arendt, *The Human Condition*, p. 40.

52 Ibid., p. 41.

53 Michel Foucault, *Discipline and Punish: The Birth of the Prison*, New York: Vintage, 1995, p. 135.

54 Arendt, *The Human Condition*, p. 49.

55 Ibid.

56 Ibid., pp. 179f.

57 Plato, *Apology*, p. 29 (31c-d).

58 Giorgio Agamben, *Profanations*, New York: Zone Books, 2007, p. 10.

59 Ibid., p. 11.

60 Ibid.

61 Ibid., p. 12.

62 Ibid. (transl. modified).

63 Arendt, *The Human Condition*, p. 134.

64 Agamben, *Profanations*, p. 11.

65 Ibid., p. 12 (transl. modified).

66 Transl. note: the German expression 'ein Fest begehen' – 'to celebrate a festival' – literally means 'to walk through a festival'.

67 Arendt, *The Human Condition*, p. 18.

68 Ibid., p. 21.

69 Ibid., p. 20. Translation modified in light of the German version; see *Vita Activa*, p. 24f.

70 Arendt, *The Human Condition*, p. 20. – Transl. note: the passage 'Life itself . . . "among human beings"' is not part of the English edition. See *Vita Activa*, p. 25.
71 Plato, *Republic*, in *Complete Works*, pp. 971–1223; here: p. 1135 (517).
72 Ibid. – Transl. note: 'it', in Plato, refers to the form of the good, 'the cause of all that is correct and beautiful in anything' (ibid.; 517b, c).
73 Arendt, *The Human Condition*, p. 525.
74 Alois M. Haas: 'Die Beurteilung der Vita contemplativa und activa in der Dominikanermystik des 14. Jahrhunderts', in Brian Vickers (ed.), *Arbeit Musse Meditation*, Zurich: Verlag der Fachvereine, 1985, pp. 109–31; here: p. 113.

The Coming Society

1 Novalis, *Philosophical Writings*, New York: State University of New York Press, 1997, p. 31.
2 Novalis, *The Disciples at Saïs*, in *The Disciples at Saïs and Other Fragments by Novalis*, London: Methuen & Co., 1903, pp. 91–143; here: p. 129 (transl. amended).
3 Friedrich Schleiermacher, *On Religion: Speeches to Its Cultured Despisers*, London: Kegan Paul, Trench, Trübner & Co., 1893, p. 277.
4 Friedrich Schleiermacher, *Über die Religion: Reden an die Gebildeten unter ihren Verächtern*, Berlin: de Gruyter, 2001, p. 68. – Transl. note: the passage is omitted in the English edition.
5 Schleiermacher, *On Religion*, p. 282 (transl. modified).
6 Friedrich Hölderlin, *Hyperion or the Hermit in Greece*, Cambridge: OpenSource Publisher, 2019, p. 8.
7 Schleiermacher, *On Religion*, pp. 100f. (transl. modified).
8 Friedrich Hölderlin, *Sämtliche Werke*, *Vol. III*, ed. F. Beissner, Stuttgart: Kohlhammer, 1958, p. 236.
9 Ibid.

10 Schleiermacher, *On Religion*, p. 277 (transl. amended).

11 Hölderlin, *Sämtliche Werke, Vol. III*, p. 236.

12 Ibid.

13 Heidegger, *Hölderlin's Hymn 'Remembrance'*, p. 150.

14 Hölderlin, *Sämtliche Werke, Vol. III*, p. 237.

15 Schleiermacher, *On Religion*, p. 56 (transl. modified).

16 Hölderlin, *Hyperion*, p. 135.

17 Schleiermacher, *Über die Religion*, p. 80. – Transl. note: the sentence is omitted in the English edition.

18 Adorno, *Aesthetic Theory*, p. 276.

19 Ibid.

20 Ibid., p. 73. – Transl. note: the full sentence continues: 'The pain in the face of beauty, nowhere more visceral than in the experience of nature, is as much the longing for what beauty promises but never unveils as it is suffering at the inadequacy of the appearance, which fails beauty while wanting to make itself like it.'

21 Heidegger, *Hölderlin's Hymn 'Remembrance'*, p. 36.

22 Friedrich Hölderlin, 'In Lovely Blueness', in *Poems and Fragments*, Ann Arbor: University of Michigan Press, 1966, pp. 601–6; here: p. 601.

23 Hölderlin, *Hyperion*, p. 81.

24 Novalis, *The Disciples at Saïs*, p. 92.

25 Ibid., p. 127.

26 Friedrich Schlegel, *Dialogue on Poetry and Literary Aphorisms*, University Park: Pennsylvania State University Press, 1968, p. 54.

27 Novalis, *Schriften, Vol. III*, Stuttgart: Kohlhammer, 1960, p. 650.

28 Oskar Walzel, *Deutsche Romantik, Vol. 1: Welt- und Kunstanschauung*, Leipzig: Teubner, 1918, p. 1.

29 Novalis, *Philosophical Writings*, p. 54.

30 Ibid.

31 Ibid.

32 Ibid., p. 56.

33 Ibid.

34 Ibid., p. 60 (transl. modified).

35 Novalis, *Henry of Ofterdingen*, Cambridge: John Owen, 1842, p. 21 ('Dedication').

36 Walter Benjamin, *One-Way Street* ('To the Planetarium'), in *Selected Writings, Vol. 1, 1913–1926*, Cambridge MA: Harvard University Press, 1996, pp. 444–88; here p. 486.

37 Novalis, 'Christendom or Europe', in *Philosophical Writings*, pp. 137–52; here: p. 152 and p. 147.

38 Ibid. p. 147.

39 Giorgio Agamben, *The Coming Community*, Minneapolis: University of Minnesota Press, 1993, p. 53.

40 Benjamin, 'In the Sun', from *Ibizan Sequence*, in *Selected Writings, Vol. 2, Part 2*, pp. 551–688; here: p. 664.

41 Novalis, *Philosophical Writings*, p. 126.

42 Novalis, *The Disciples at Saïs*, p. 93.